S0-BYM-301

Features

PAGE 4

PAGE 16

PAGE 20

PAGE 32

PAGE 56

PAGE 66

PAGE 76

PAGE 80

Departments

Publisher
Louis Weber

Associate Publisher
Estelle Weber

Publications Director
Frank E. Peiler

Editor in Chief
Chris Poole

Associate Editor
Rick Popely

Special Projects Editor
Roland Flessner

Production Editor
Mark McIntyre

Assistant Publications Director: Mona Syring **Acquisitions Editor:** David V. Stuart **Production Manager:** David Darian **Production Director:** Susan St. Onge **Editorial Assistants:** Amy Okrei, Gert Salzenstein, Kathy OKrei, Mickey Zivin, Shirley Weiner **Art Direc-**tor: Frank E. Peiler **Art Department Manager:** Brenda Kaharl **Art Assistants:** Barbara Clemens, Janet Fuglsang, Terese Kolodziej, Deborah McCaslin **Photographers:** Bud Juneau, David Gooley, Sam Griffith, Doug Mitchel **President:** Louis Weber **Executive Vice President:** Estelle Weber **Vice Presidents:** Frank E. Peiler, Steven Feinberg **Vice President, Advertising:** Jay L. Butler **Marketing Director:** Dan Blau **Circulation Manager:** Edward Geraghty

Advertising Sales Office
225 W. 34th St., Suite 806
New York, NY 10122
(212) 564-7007

Editorial and Subscription Offices
3841 W. Oakton St.
Skokie, IL 60076
(312) 676-3470

Copyright © 1984 by Publications International, Ltd. All rights reserved. This magazine may not be reproduced or quoted in whole or in part by mimemograph or any other printed means or for presentation on radio, television, videotape, or film without written permission from Louis Weber, President of Publications International, Ltd. Permission is never granted for commercial purposes. Printed in USA, Collectible Automobile is published six times a year.

What Makes a Collectible Automobile?

It's usually best to begin something at the beginning, especially if it's new. So—first of all—WELCOME to *Collectible Automobile*.™ We thought it would be appropriate to tell you about our editorial plans, which partly explains the double meaning of the title. So before we get into what distinguishes a collectible automobile from other cars, a few words about what distinguishes *Collectible Automobile*™ from other car magazines.

For one thing, it arrives with a great deal of experience and acclaim behind it, for it comes to you from the auto editors of CONSUMER GUIDE® Publications. Since 1978, we've produced dozens of books and magazines on a broad range of cars, written primarily for enthusiasts. The titles run the gamut from Pontiacs to Porsches, and include the enormously popular *Encyclopedia of American Cars 1940-1970*, widely hailed as one of the all-time best buys in its field and still the most authoritative, easiest to use book of its kind.

Our pioneering *Complete Book of Collectible Cars 1940-1980* was the inspiration for this new bimonthly, which will have the same hallmarks of honesty, brevity, and a wealth of information. Unlike so many "buff books" we don't intend to bore you with a lot of rambling words, nor will we be content to rehash the same old stories you've read a dozen times before. And we will not simply wax nostalgic or repeat often-heard falsehoods about particular models, even the "great" ones. In assessing collectibility we intend to be critical and hardnosed about a car's basic design and its desirability as a financial investment. This means we'll point out both the pros *and* cons with respect to asking prices, parts availability, restoration problems, appreciation potential, and other areas affecting you, the owner or potential owner. In short, our editorial goals are to be balanced and objective as well as entertaining and informative.

We also intend *Collectible Automobile*™ to be the class act in this field. Thumb through this inaugural issue and you'll see authors whose names and expertise are well known. Check the gorgeous color photography, the work of top-notch professionals. You'll find page after page of it in *every* issue of *Collectible Automobile.*™ That's a promise.

Our dedication to excellence is also reflected in the magazine's regular departments. Besides the usual events calendar and book reviews you'll find fascinating facts in Collectible Scale Automobile and Collectible Automobilia that will expand your horizons

as a hobbyist. The thought-provoking Cheap Wheels section examines interesting older models that can be realistic alternatives to modern cars as daily transportation—just the thing for those who want to drive something different. In Future Collectibles our experts look at the cars of the present and recent past to see which ones are likely to be collected—and to go up in value—in the years ahead. Controversial we expect it to be, but the mystery is why no one's done this before. And in future issues we plan to look at the collectibility of neoclassics like the Excalibur as well as restored street rods and customs, which are already starting to attract a great deal of attention in the hobby.

Now that you know about the magazine, what about the cars you'll see in it? In the main, our emphasis in the historical articles and Photo Features will be on the post-World War II American models that today command the bulk of collector/enthusiast interest. However, we'll also regularly highlight cars of the '30s and early '40s, plus a number of desirable models from the better-known foreign manufacturers.

But let's go back to our title question: what makes a collectible automobile? Chances are you already have your own answers—along with every other living car enthusiast. And that's part of the problem. While we could all probably agree that not every older car is worth preserving, deciding which ones are and which ones aren't can be a highly subjective matter, one that leads to heated debate and sometimes inexplicable rises or falls in the prices of cars branded "collectible."

So, let's agree to disagree. Any list of "great" cars is subject to debate, and few people will agree completely on which cars should be on it. And that's fine with us.

Let's agree on another fact of life: even the "great" cars aren't perfect. The Model T, for all its charm and historical significance, is hardly a dream to drive. The imposing Duesenberg SJ, for all its charisma and power, is hardly easy to buy nowadays, let alone find. The much newer Cosworth-Vega, despite its small numbers and race-linked engineering, is still after all a Vega, with all that implies for desirability—or lack thereof.

Can we also agree on two more points? One is that the basic qualities that make any automobile worth saving are those that make a collectible anything, whether it's a piece of furniture, a painting, or a set of baseball cards. The second is that, as collectibles, cars are somehow special. They tend to evoke very personal emotions and memories in people from all walks of life, including those who don't even care much about

The 1936 Cord 810 Westchester sedan

automobiles and many who don't care much about collecting anything. Often the response is nostalgia ("I used to own one of those"). Sometimes it's wonderment ("You mean cars actually had pushbutton transmissions once?"). For car enthusiasts, these may be coupled with a kind of abstract appreciation of styling or engineering, or perhaps a model's commercial success or failure (the last explains the longtime fascination with the Edsel, for instance). So, the criteria used to judge an automobile as collectible differ somewhat from those applied to other objects. But what are these and can they be applied with any reasonable consistency and logic?

Here are our answers. There are five basic factors: rarity (low production), exceptionally good—or exceptionally bad—styling and/or engineering, historical significance (e.g., innovative design, first or last of the line, etc.), performance, and craftsmanship. Again, enthusiasts will argue over the *degree* to which a given model scores in these areas, but there's no doubt that the more of them it satisfies the more collectible the car. We also think cars can be evaluated logically

"Not every older car is worth preserving; deciding which ones are and which ones aren't is a highly subjective matter."

and consistently this way—*if* you have a non-partisan judge. That we will try to be. Nostalgia and collector esteem may be helpful in identifying cars that might be collectible, but they aren't very objective. Neither are such things as sales performance, contemporary press opinion, or even current market activity.

So there you have it: where we stand on collectible automobiles and what we plan to do with *Collectible Automobile.*™ We're all very excited about our new creation, and we hope you'll like it enough to become one of our regular subscribers. Contrary to the old axiom, imitation is not the sincerest form of flattery. It's appreciation.

Chris Poole

1958 Chevrolet Impala: The Forgotten Hot One

The first Impala should have been a sought-after collector's item years ago. It has all the necessary qualities—including performance—plus distinction as a one-year-only design.

by Pat Chappell

Model year 1983 marked a significant event in automotive history: the 25th birthday of the first Chevrolet Impala. Yet there were no splashy retrospectives in the "buff books" to mark the occasion, not even so much as a press release from Chevrolet Division. Considering the Impala nameplate has probably been found in more driveways than any other in the years since, this apparent widespread indifference is curious.

But things are changing. The 1958 Impala is at last being recognized for the collectible automobile it is. A growing number of enthusiasts are turning to these cars, and there's now even a club, called '58 Impalas Ltd.,

devoted exclusively to them. These people didn't forget the car's birthday, and the club had a special window sticker printed up so others wouldn't either. Surrounding the now-familiar insignia with the fleet African antelope striding above Chevy's crossed flags are the simple words: "Happy 25th Anniversary. '58 Was Worth the Wait."

It's logical to ask why the wait has been such a long one, because the '58 Impala should have been a sought-after collector's item long ago. Consider its credentials. For starters, there's its historical significance as the first of what would be an amazingly successful model line, bearing a name

4

that would become almost synonymous with Chevrolet itself for millions of motorists. Then, too, the original Impala shared with lesser '58 Chevys the distinction of a unique one-year-only body design. Moreover—and contrary to conventional mythology—the Impala was not just a trim option in its first year but a structurally different model, with equipment and special body panels not found on other '58 Chevys. It was, of course, the new top-of-the-line offering that year, available exclusively in the two body styles most favored by collectors, convertible—the only one in the line, incidentally—and two-door hardtop coupe.

Top: This beautifully restored '58 Impala convertible, owned by Jim Heidenway, was one of 55,989 built. Above: Impala side trim was inspired by Ghia's '54 Fiat V-8 coupe.

MADLER
3-15-56

13337

6

The Impala also represented something new for Chevy, the division's first-ever attempt to break out of the low-price field and into the lower end of the medium segment. As such, it was a smash. With production of 125,480 coupes and 55,989 convertibles, the Impala accounted for fully 15 percent of Chevy's 1958 model year output, and helped the division capture 30 percent of the market for the first time in its history. That's fair going in a recession year when car sales fell to barely 4.5 million from six million plus the year before, and with the jobless rate soaring to 7.7 percent, a 16-year peak.

Opposite page, top: Corvette Impala show car of 1956 provided a hint of the all-new '58 standard Chevys. Below: Grille teeth were ruled out as too expensive, so front-end workouts proceeded around a combination bumper/grille. Basic Impala lines were almost final by mid-March 1956. This page: Stock restorations today tend to be loaded with accessories, as Wayne Essary's pristine convertible amply demonstrates.

But the question remains: why has the first Impala been so long forgotten? Part of the answer is the "classic" Chevys that preceeded it, cars that had already gained a measure of enthusiast esteem even as the '58s were introduced. The overwhelming interest in the 1955-57 models that developed in the years since continues to this day, and it has simply pushed most every other Chevy of this era into the shadows, the Corvettes and the later Impala Super Sports being notable exceptions. The other part of the answer is what the Impala became in later years: "the mid-century American Anycar," as one wag put it. The name and its initial exclusivity were watered down the very next year, 1959, when it was extended to sedans and four-door hardtops to create a new top-end series displacing Bel Air. This line would go on to become the country's top-selling nameplate in the '60s and, as it did so, enthusiasts' memories of the glamorous original dimmed. By

the end of the decade the Impala had been eclipsed by the Caprice as Chevy's finest, and the interesting Super Sports had vanished. The name would be further diluted in the '70s. Today, it barely survives on a single price-leader four-door in the full-size line.

There's also this: for all its merits as a collectible, the 1958 Impala is not without flaws. Perhaps the biggest one is that it was *not* one of the agile, spirited, well-built "Hot Ones." After these cars, all the '58 Chevys must have seemed disappointing despite an all-new—and generally much-improved—design. They were larger and heavier, of course—few cars that year weren't—and acceleration and roadability suffered. The accent was now strictly on soft-riding luxury, flashy styling, and Buick-like proportions, precisely those things the Impala had been designed for. Another black mark for collectors is the generally lower standard of workmanship on the '58s—though Chevy was hardly alone in this at the time—and the cars were definitely rust-prone. The new styling was conservative in a generally garish year but has always been controversial. Finally, there was Chevy's new 348-cid big-block V-8. It promised much, but was sneered at for having started out as a truck engine. Never mind that it served as the basis for the "real fine" 409 mill a few years afterwards. It was hardly the sort of follow-up expected after the sophisticated, high-winding 265/283 small-block.

What all this adds up to is that a much smaller percentage of '58 Chevys—Impalas included—have been saved relative to total production, which itself has tended to reinforce collector disinterest. It's fortunate that at least the Impalas are now being saved from extinction, for this is an interesting car both technically and historically.

Work on the 1958 design began in June 1955 at a meeting of Chevrolet styling chief Clare MacKichan, Pontiac's studio heads, and the GM body design committee. Pontiac was in on this because it would share the Chevy's new A-body. The consensus was the '58s should be larger—longer, wider, and heavier—and much lower. This proved to be a key decision for Chevrolet and one that would affect other automakers, too. After all, if the top seller did something, the rest of the industry was bound to follow sooner or later. GM's desire to move Chevy away from the 115-inch wheelbase of 1955-57 toward luxury-car size was logical. Detroit was having a record-breaking sales year in '55, with medium-price makes scoring the largest gains, and product planners concluded the market would trend steadily upward in the years ahead. It was this reasoning, of course, that led Ford to bring out its ill-starred Edsel.

Accordingly, the '58 Chevrolet would be bigger and better, completely different from anything the division had offered before. And it would be virtually all-new from the ground up: new body, new chassis, a larger optional V-8, and a new all-coil suspension designed to permit installation of optional airbag springs. What few could foresee in '55 was that this car would last but a single year. Some time ago we asked MacKichan

The '58 Chevrolet would be bigger and better, completely different from anything the division had offered before. And it would be virtually all new from the ground up.

A handsome example of the '58 Impala Sport Coupe, owned by John Cox. Proportions on this model differed from those on the equivalent Bel Air, with a slightly shorter greenhouse and correspondingly longer rear deck. Chrome rocker moldings and the "pitchfork" dummy rear fender scoops were unique to Impalas among '58 Chevrolets.

why the '58 styling was killed so quickly. He explained: "In 1959 we went to a shared bodyshell with Pontiac, Oldsmobile, and Buick. This was an effort to save money in the corporation. The idea was to make the outer surfaces different so that nobody would know they were shared, but the things underneath that cost the major amount of money *would* be shared."

Chevy's '58 styling was hinted at by two Motorama show cars, the Corvette Impala, a two-door hardtop shown in 1956, and the Biscayne, a hardtop sedan seen the year before. More rounded and "formed" than GM's then-current production models, they were mainly the creation of Chevy studio designer Jerry Cumbus, and influenced much of the styling development for the 1958 program. The experimental Impala's front end featured a Corvette-like vertical-bar motif, a theme strongly favored for the '58s, but it was axed in favor of a combination bumper/grille because of cost reasons. The latter made for styling continuity with the '57 Chevy, but wasn't as distinctive as the 'Vette's "teeth."

Early on in the '58 program, Chevy planners had envisioned a "super" Bel Air model that would be quite different from the rest of the line and not just a fancy trim package. Originally called "Bel Air Executive Coupe," it became the focal point for much of the styling effort. Eventually it was retitled Impala, a name chosen to connote grace and speed.

The production Impala was indeed quite "special" compared with other '58 Chevys. For example, the Sport Coupe roofline was different from that on the Bel Air hardtops, shorter and marked by a curved contour crease at the rear ending in a chrome dummy air scoop, a direct "lift" of the functional air extractor vents on the Mercedes-Benz 300SL Gullwing. Another European touch was the prominent sidespear body moldings inspired by the '54 Fiat V-8 coupe designed by Ghia of Italy. All '58s had these, but the Impala's entire lower body was different. Everything from the A-pillar back—doors, decklid, rear fender extensions—were not interchangeable. And though the Impala hardtop had the same length and width as other Chevys, it had differ-

ent proportions, with a longer rear deck and a correspondingly shorter cabin giving it a more close-coupled look. Other distinctions on both Impala models included special wheel covers, stainless-steel rocker panel trim, and chrome moldings ahead of the rear wheel openings intended to simulate rear-facing air scoops. These are sometimes called "pitchforks" due to their shape. The Impala's two-toning was more conservative than on other models, too, with the contrasting color appearing only on the coupe's roof or the convertible's folding top. This served to focus attention on the lower body, with its sculptured "shoulders" sweeping back to the canted "gullwing" fins. These wrapped around the individual round taillamps on all models, but the Impala was again unique in using three lights instead of two.

The Impala's interior was created by Ed Donaldson, chief of Chevy's interior studio, and carried many reminders that this model was Chevy's best. The driver faced a competition-inspired two-spoke steering wheel with simulated lightening holes and Impala medallion on the hub. Impala

Opposite page and right: Two-toning on '58 Impala convertibles was limited strictly to a contrasting top, keyed to the primary body color. Styling on the '58 Chevys was conservative and tasteful compared to cars from other GM divisions that season.

script adorned the dash, which had a lower rail vee'd around the steering column, thus echoing the gullwing shape of the rear fenders. Exclusive to the Impala were colored-keyed door panels with brushed-aluminum trim, and horizontal-stripe upholstery available in three shades keyed to exterior paint. The back seat featured a pull-down armrest in the center below a radio speaker grille, the latter adorned with Impala emblems.

All the '58 Chevys were as much changed mechanically as they were in appearance. A new X-type frame was adopted, which allowed stylists to lower overall height by some five inches compared to the '57s without sacrificing interior space, ground clearance, or torsional strength. In fact, this new all-welded structure, designed by engineers Ed Cole and Harry Barr, was reportedly 30-percent stronger than the ladder-type chassis previously used. Some felt this predicted the advent of unit construction. Because the new chassis had no side rails, the body rocker panels had to be very strong, which made for considerably tighter assembly.

Dimensionally the '58 Chevys were right in step with the times. Wheelbase was up 2.5 inches to 117.5, overall length was up by a full 9 inches to 209 inches, and curb weight ballooned by 200-300 pounds compared to the '57s. Enthusiasts have often criticized the '58s for being needlessly big and heavy, but it should be pointed out that both Ford and Plymouth had moved away from their 1955-56 "midsize" designs the year before, and Chevy was doing nothing more than catching up with its competitors in the "space race."

Chevy's suspension was completely new for '58, with coils substituting for leafs at the rear and a second pair of trailing arms was added to locate the live axle. The lower arms were mounted to the frame, while the upper ones were attached either side of the axle housing. Chevy called this "four-link" suspension, and claimed improved handling and shock absorber action for it. Up front were the traditional coil springs and

wishbones. With all this, the '58 Chevy had a higher roll center, lower center of gravity, and a softer ride with the same stability as before. It really was a great advance in suspension design.

Chevy also attended to engines this year. The trusty 235-cid "Blue Flame" six was still around, as was the 283 small-block V-8 offered with various carburetion setups or optional Ramjet fuel injection. But the real news was a larger 348-cid V-8, called "Turbo Thrust" to distinguish it from the "Turbo Fire" small-blocks.

This new powerplant, designed by John T. Rausch with assistance from Howard Kehrl and Donald McPherson, had started life as the Type W engine, and was originally intended primarily for truck use. But it was the only engine available to Chevy for its larger, heavier '58s, and it got the job done. Its combustion chambers were of the cylindrical wedge shape, formed by flat-bottom heads that rested on the block faces at a 16-degree angle. Pistons were of cast aluminum, machined with 16-degree dual-sloping surfaces. Lifters were oversize with hydraulic actuation, and dual exhausts were standard. With its 4.84-inch cylinder spacing, the 348 had much more room for future enlargement than the maximum 302 cid allowed by the small-block and its then-current crankshaft, and it would go on to be the basis of the legendary 409, introduced in mid-1961. On a 4.125-inch bore and 3.25-inch stroke, the 348 was tuned to deliver 250 bhp in standard form. An optional Power Pack raised output to

280 bhp via three dual-throat carbs with progressive linkage and 9.5:1 compression.

In either guise, this engine made any '58 Chevy quite quick—maybe not as fast as the "fuelie" 283 in a '57, but fast enough to qualify definitely as one of the "Hot Ones." Dick Reddy tested a 250-bhp Bel Air four-door hardtop for Dell Publishing's 1958 buyers guide, and ran the 0-60 mph sprint in a respectable 9.9 seconds. Top-end speed was 115 mph with the new Turboglide automatic (of which more shortly), 50-70 mph highway passing took just 5.9 seconds, and mileage was pegged at 12-18 mpg of premium. *Motor Trend* did even better: 9.1 seconds 0-60 mph and 16.5 seconds for the standing quarter-mile with its 280-bhp Impala coupe.

Reddy also drove an Impala coupe with the big-block mill, Turboglide, and 3.36:1 Positraction rear axle, and his comments are illuminating: "I aimed the Impala's horns down the fairway and pressed the loud pedal all the way down. The response, while not breath-catching, was far above average, and we left a bit of rubber before the excellent rear wheel traction bit in and snapped us away. I had a feeling that [weight distribution] was just about right, heavier enough in front to keep the front end from breaking first in a fast bend, yet not so heavy that the rear floated behind like the tail of a kite...So far as I'm concerned, Chevrolet has put the torque [355 lbs/ft] right where it belongs....From 0 to 70 it will do anything you demand of it, picking up without noise or protest at the lightest pedal pressure. Above 70 you are conscious that you are out of the car's favorite range, but there is still plenty there, all the way up to 100 and beyond." If that's not performance, we don't know what is.

No report on the '58 Chevys would be complete without mention of two optional features new this year, "Level Air" suspension and Turboglide automatic transmission. Both appeared before they were fully developed, proved unreliable, and vanished after only a few years. Also, both were quite expensive given the state of the national economy, and neither was really necessary.

Level Air, of course, was Chevy's response to the Detroit air suspension fad that had begun the year before. The system comprised four bell-shaped rubber bellows, one at each wheel, plus an engine-driven air compressor and reserve air tank mounted up front. The bellows, responding to changes in road surface, were automatically adjusted by the compressor in response to wheel motion. Level Air did provide less nose-dive in heavy braking and a more stable ride than the conventional all-coil setup; also ride attitude was less noticeably affected by heavy loads in the trunk. Trouble was, it didn't work reliably. One writer summed up Level Air this way: "Air might be free, but the system was costly [$124], offered few advantages over conventional springing, and broke down." Interest in air suspensions peaked almost as soon as it began, and Level Air was ordered on only a few thousand '58 Chevys. Altogether, only about 100,000 cars were built with air suspension for '58, just two percent of production. In Chevy's case, the new chassis didn't really need Level Air, even if it had worked as promised, and the option would disappear from the catalog by 1960. Said one observer: "Detroit got caught following the leader and the leader went down a blind alley."

Turboglide automatic had originated in 1957 as a luxury option to supplement the familiar two-speed Powerglide transmission. It, too, would be short-lived, making its last stand in 1961, with Powerglide continuing until the advent of Turbo-Hydramatic at Chevy for 1965. Created by engineers Oliver Kelly and Frank Winchell, Turboglide was a

five-element, geared-converter-type transmission, priced at $231 for '58 against Powerglide's $188 tariff. Although Ken Fermoyle of *Motor Life* magazine and Walt Woron of *Motor Trend* had some good things to say about it, Turboglide turned out to be a nightmare for both customers and mechanics, prone to failure and difficult at best to repair. Too bad, because according to *Mechanix Illustrated's* road test dean, Tom McCahill, when working properly "it is as smooth as velvet underpants."

In the 1970s we asked Vince Piggins, long-time manager for Chevrolet's Production Promotion department, about the necessity for Turboglide. His assessment: "We had the Powerglide, which was a very successful transmission, and we also had the Hydra-Matic, which not only GM but American Motors was using. So there was really very little need of another transmission, and it was expensive to build. It wasn't as economical as the Hydra-Matic because it was a two-speed, much like the Buick Dynaflow." In retrospect, said Piggins, "it would have taken a few more years to really get Turboglide to the reliability stage that the Hydra-Matic already achieved and, sales being what they were, it just didn't make sense."

Road testers generally liked the '58 Chevys as much as buyers did, the Impala in particular. Most reports commented favorably on the com-

Above: Brushed-aluminum door panel trim and horizontal-stripe upholstery were unique to Impala for '58, as shown on this convertible. Owner: Jim Heidenway. Opposite page: Impala lost its initial exclusivity after just one year, becoming the new top-line series for the radically styled "bat-wing" '59 line. Shown is Don Ruhff's immaculate Impala Sport Coupe.

fortable front seat and driving position, excellent outward vision, and well-laid-out instrument panel. Brakes were usually judged good in normal use, but were prone to fade in high-speed stops. The car was "commendably" stable in a straight line, though understeer was marked in tight turns, and the steering was criticized as needing excessive wheel-twirling, though the turning circle was actually tighter than on the '57s. The ride was medium-firm, and body roll was well-controlled. Mileage wasn't as good as before, especially with the big-block engine, and the car wasn't as nimble, either. *Motor Trend*

matched up the Impala against a 305-bhp Plymouth Fury and a 300-bhp Ford Fairlane 500 hardtop. While the magazine avoided picking a winner, the comments of driver Russ Kelly should be noted: "The Impala should easily win acceptance from the sports-minded automobile enthusiast. It's a solid car, with good cornering characteristics, plenty of power, and a chassis that should hold up under a rugged life...Check your needs as to carrying more than one adult passenger; the rear seat is not adequate...for long trips. Check your pocketbook as regards your outlay for gasoline. Check your local traffic and highway conditions, for with the Impala you'll want to drive fast." Said Dick Reddy: "The new Chevy should make a lot of new converts to the Old Firm. It certainly won't lose any of the old customers."

It's easy to get upset about the first Impala. Some have blamed it for the pernicious trend to bigger and bigger low-priced cars that blossomed in the '60s—for steering Detroit from the nimble, middle-sized package of the mid-'50s to behemoths of little merit or distinction. Certainly the '58 Impala was the direct opposite of the "classic" Chevys in concept, but it was right in step with the market and, as noted, it sold well. In fact, it solidified Chevy's sales position in a year that bordered on disaster for the industry as a whole. And it was a brand-new design—one of the few really

fresh and tasteful ones—in a year that needed every assist because of the flagging economy. This was of great importance to Chevrolet, and the Impala helped the division prepare for a spectacular recovery in the '60s. "Many people at the time thought the design was good," remembered stylist Carl Renner. "However, there were those who referred to the rear fenders as World War I barrage balloons due to their shape and fullness. It was the first suggestion of a concave fin, leading into the larger fin of 1959. But I think it was a successful car for the time."

And for our time, too. Forget philosophy, consider the Forgotten Hot One simply as a car, and you'll find a great many redeeming qualities. It may have taken 25 years, but the first Impala will be forgotten no longer.

Special thanks to photographers Bert Johnson, Bud Juneau, and Douglas Mitchel for their Impala portraits. The author thanks the following for their help in preparing this article: Ed Bittman; David Brownell, editor of Special-Interest Autos *magazine; Bob Chauvin, Can Am Restoration Supply; Jeff Cramer, '58 Impalas, Ltd.; John Gunnell and Tony Hossain, Krause Publications; Wick Humble; Kathy Johnson, Ciadella Enterprises, Inc.; Richard M. Langworth; Ed Reavie; Jeannie and Robert Ripley; Robert Snowden, Late Great Chevrolet Association; Don Trivett, Volunteer State Chevy Parts; and Tom Whipple, T&N Supply. Special thanks to*

Charles M. Jordan, Director of Design, GM Design Staff and to Floyd Joliet, Design Staff Administrative Operations, for '58 Chevrolet styling development photography.

Clubs for 1958 Chevrolet Impalas

Late Great Chevrolet Association
P.O. Box 17824
Orlando, FL 32860

National Impala Association
1752 South Boulevard
Idaho Falls, IA 83401

Veteran Motor Car Club
105 Elm Street
Andover, MA 01810

Vintage Chevrolet Club of America
P.O. Box 5387
Orange, CA 92667

1958 Chevrolet Impala Collector's Guide

No question about it: the 1958 Chevrolet Impala has arrived as a collectible automobile. There's also no question that it's *the* prime collectible among all '58 Chevys. The Impala's obvious attractions are at last being appreciated (see accompanying story), so the main questions left to answer here relate to prices, investment potential, and restoration problems.

Until very recently you could buy one of these cars for little more than a song, anywhere from $1000 for a clapped-out coupe to $8000 or so for a mint-condition ragtop. Now, growing recognition within the hobby is pushing prices inexorably upward. One guide lists $10,000 as the typical figure for a nice, original Sport Coupe and $13,000 for a convertible in similar condition. However, there seems to be more interest at present in *restored*, not original, examples, which cost more than original-condition cars but tend to sell for less than the combined cost of buying a car and then rebuilding it. Reliable sources have told us that costs for a 100-point "body-off-the-frame" restoration on a '58 Impala could easily equal the above vehicle prices. Thus, today's buyer benefits in a way from the car's long years of neglect by the hobby, which has tended to depress values for both original and restored specimens. As the first Impala continues to gain recognition, you can expect sellers of restored cars to try to recoup their costs much more adamantly than they have in the past.

If the Impala's prices are now in flux, so is its investment potential. A few years ago, knowledgeable sources pegged it at about 25 percent over a five-year period. Right now we're inclined to boost that by 5 to 10 points, partly on the strength of the model's new-found collector interest and partly because the cars are sure to become scarcer as time goes by.

At the very least, the car's future within the hobby is bright. Right now there are five national clubs that welcome the '58 Impala and can supply owners with a wealth of information on parts sources, restoration assistance, and availability of cars, plus friendly camaraderie. And it seems only a matter of time before the Impala will be eligible for Antique Automobile Club of America certification (that group's cut-off is 1957 models at this writing; '58s will be added in 1984).

After years of near invisibility, the Impala is now seen more and more often at shows. Because it lends itself readily to both stock and modified restoration, it has become popular with enthusiasts of all ages, just like its vaunted 1955-57 predecessors. Stock specimens tend to be loaded to the hilt with factory accessories, so prospective buyers should be on the lookout for items like continental kit, twin rear fender antennas, factory fender skirts, and the signal-seeking "Wonder Bar" AM radio. Custom jobs are usually done in a very early-'60s style, sporting items popular in that era such as cruiser skirts, tubular grilles, '59 Cadillac taillamps, lake pipes, and tuck-and-roll upholstery.

Parts availability is a mixed bag at present. Some new-old stock is still available, but sources are drying up rapidly. Again reflecting the greater popularity of the 1955-57 Chevys, there aren't nearly as many reproduction '58 parts around. Those that have been marketed are mostly trim items, including some upholstery and interior panels, miscellaneous rubber parts, dash pads and faceplates, taillight assemblies, rocker panel moldings, trunk mats, wheel spinners, and assorted emblems and ornaments.

Sheetmetal presents a special restoration problem because of the very individuality that makes the '58 Impala so desirable in the first place. All '58 Chevys were rust-prone in the headlight area, lower front fenders, rocker panels, rear wheel wells, lower rear quarters, and trunk floor. The only solution is to replace any damaged areas with rust-free sections welded in place. The problem is finding the new metal. It's less difficult for areas forward of the A-pillar, since the Impala shared its front end with other '58 Chevys. But if the repair lies anywhere from the cowl back, the new metal will have to come from another Impala, and one can only imagine how few good examples are left to be found in junkyards. Remember that only 181,000 of the '58s were produced, and our best guess is that only about one fourth (45,000) have survived in anything like useable form. It may be less than that and for a simple reason: enthusiasts just haven't been interested in saving *any* '58 Chevys—even Impalas—until recently.

No doubt a good many restorers will rise above these difficulties to preserve their cars and certain of its features, like the Level Air suspension, the Turboglide transmission, perhaps even the 280-bhp Turbo Thrust V-8 with three-twos under the hood. Like the many 1955-57 restorations that have gone before, these '58s will surely be completed to perfection and operable in every way, as God and Chevrolet Division intended. Time can only enhance the appeal of this late-bloomer collectible, and we predict that growing enthusiasm for the '58 Impala will stimulate a much larger number of reproduction parts including, we hope, that hard to find sheetmetal. The Forgotten Hot One deserves no less.

Below: Wayne Essary's '58 ragtop looks like something from Chevy's accessory catalog.

FROM ALBION SCOTT

MOTOBOOKS

CALL TOLL-FREE 1-800-654-6505 or 212-980-1928/9 in NY

THE FINEST IN MOTORING LITERATURE
10% DISCOUNT ON ORDERS OVER $150

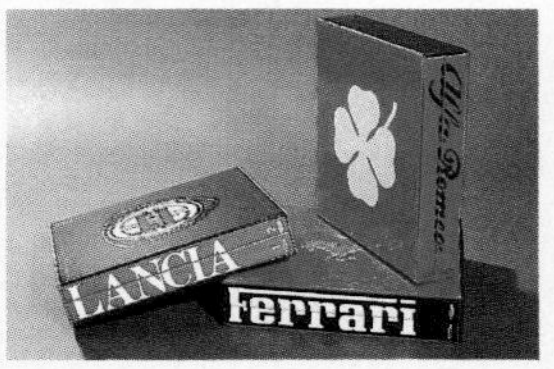

CATALOG RAISONNEE SERIES: FERRARI CATALOGUE-2ND EDITION This is the complete model catalogue for the years 1946-1981 in 2 volumes, protected by a handsome slipcase. Together the books contain over 1000 photographs, 48 color pictures and 7 watercolors, with a text in English, French and Italian. Each of the 260 models produced by Ferrari are described with pictures, technical data and technical drawings. Also details history of Ferrari, designers, and lists drivers and races won. Now available in the corrected 2nd edition. A true collectors item **$149.50**

ALFA ROMEO CATALOGUE by L. Fusi and G. Lurani. This massive 2-volume work covers all aspects of the cars and the company with each section being written by an acknowledged expert. Text in English, French and Italian, slipcased. 10″×11-1/4″, 550 pp, 1000 b/w ill., 24 color plates **$149.50**

LANCIA CATALOGUE by F. Bernabo. The definitive reference work on Lancia, covering the entire history since 1907 in 2 volumes. Includes company history, tech and component specs by model, plus racing program. Also features an enormous photo collection showing every production and racing car built by Lancia. 2 vols, slipcased, 9-1/2″×11″, 550 pp, 1000 ill., 32 color plates. **$175.00**

In the same series (available soon):
LAMBORGHINI CATALOGUE $175.00; MERCEDES BENZ CATALOGUE $175.00

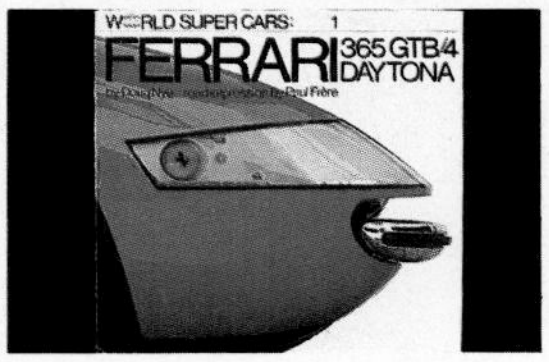

WORLD SUPERCAR SERIES: FERRATI DAYTONA 36-GTB-4 by Doug Nye & Paul Frere. (not actual cover) This full color portrait of one of the most desirable Ferrari models covers the Ferrari heritage, the V12 engine, the genesis of the Daytona, an assessment of the car including comparisons with similar super-cars, competition history, road tests, the number and location of surviving cars and information on car clubs, specialists and restorers. Hb, 88 pp, 60 color and 30 b/w pictures (approx.) **$16.95**

LAMBORGHINI COUNTACH-LP 400, LP500S by Jeremy Coulter. J. Coulter, longtime enthusiast and expert, takes us through the genesis of the car. Including predecessors, such as the Miura, comparisons with contemporary rivals. Contains many color photos, engine details and full technical specs. 88 pp, hb, 60 color, 30 b/w ill. (approx.) **$16.95**

You will find MOTOBOOKS branches in London, Bewdley (Worcs.), Brussels, Antwerp, Tel Aviv, Dusseldorf, Hamburg, Frankfurt, Berlin, Helsinki.

SPECIAL OFFER: THE SPIRIT by Ken Dallison. 24 original lithographs of Rolls Royces in period settings, each illustration printed on heavy art stock, 18″×14″. Foreword by Lord Montague, descriptions of the illustrated models, covers sheathed in Conolly Vaumol leather, removeable bindings (permits framing). Each portfolio signed and numbered by the artist, limited edition of 2000 portfolios. On continuous exhibition at the Royal Mews in the UK. Originally published at $600.00, now only **$195.00** (limited quantity available, order now).

THE GREAT AMERICAN CLASSICS by Ken Dallison. 24 original lithographs of American Classics in period settings (20's and 30's). Foreword by Otis Chandler, editor of LA Times. Descriptions of the models, covers sheathed in top-grain American cowhide, removeable binding. Limited edition of 2000 portfolios, each signed and numbered by the artist. Originally published at $600.00, now only **$195.00** (limited quantity, order now).

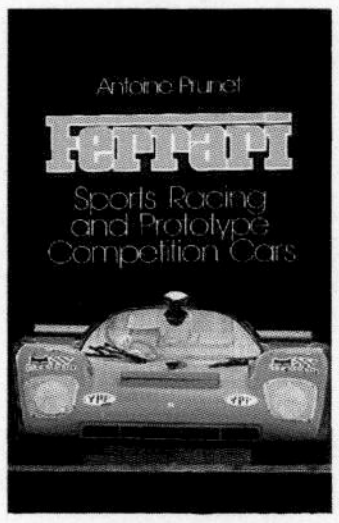

THE FERRARI LEGEND: SPORTS RACING AND PROTOTYPE COMPETITION CARS by Antoine Prunet. Details the entire history from 1947-1973 with well researched text and hundred's of pictures. 46 page all color section. Hb, 430 pp **$50.00**

BUGATTI by Hugh Conway and Jacques Greilsamer. A very lavish illustrated history of Bugatti. A section is devoted to each type. Includes 500 diagrams and 170 color illustrations. Reproductions of all original sales catalogues. Many original documents, technical tables and production data. Text and captions are in French and English. 2nd and enlarged edition. Hb, slipcased, 12½″×9½″, 304 pp, 200 b/w and 170 color ill. **$79.95**

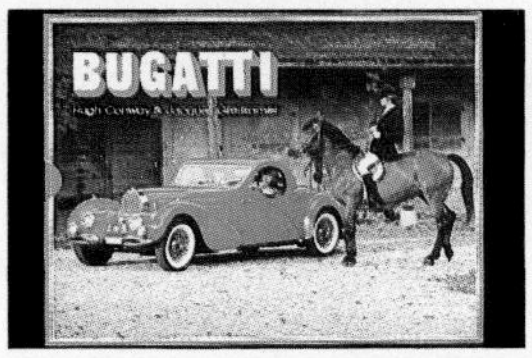

ROLLS ROYCE AUTO-HISTORIES–Strong pictorial coverage and high overall quality have gained this series a fantastic reputation. Approx. 80 b/w and 12 color photos plus authoritative text highlight the various models. Hb, 7½″×8½″, 136 pp.

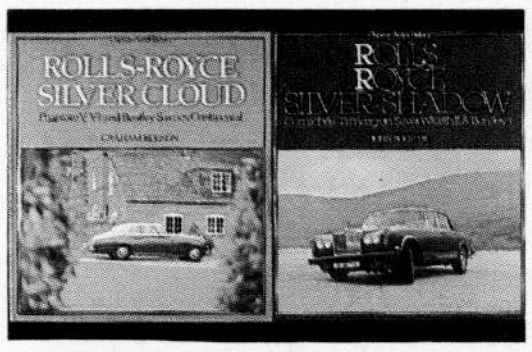

Rolls Royce Silver Cloud by G. Robson. Covers Silver Cloud from the late 40's to the mid 60's plus Phantom & the Bentley S and Continental series **$14.95**

Rolls Royce Silver Shadow by John Bolster. Covers Silver Shadow, Corniche, Camargue, Silver Wraith 2 and Bentley T. **$14.95**

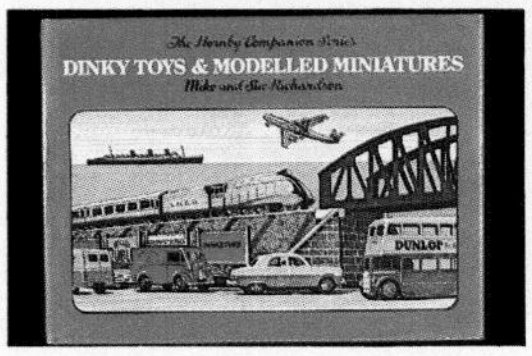

DINKY TOYS AND MODELED MINIATURES by Mike and Sue Richardson. This is a comprehensive history of all known Dinky Toy production from 1933-1979. Much material from the factory archives including original design drawings. A vast book of nostalgia and information, plus a fantastic reference source. Vol. 4 in the Hornby Companion series. Hb, 11¼″×8½″, 312 pp, over 700 ill., 350 in color **$59.95**

FROM OUR VAST BACKLIST

ALFA ROMEO
- **Alfa Romeo Giulietta** 176 pp., 130 ill . . . $29.95
- **Alfa Romeo 1900** Print (It. text) . . . $29.95
- **Alfa Spiders Autohistory** 90+ ill. . . . $14.95

AUSTIN HEALEY
- **Healey Handsome Brute** by Harvey . . . $29.95
- **Sprites & Midgets Coll. Guide** . . . $18.95
- **Big Healeys Coll. Guide** . . . $18.95
- **Healey Autocar** . . . $17.95

BMW
- **BMW Complete Story from 1928** . . . $29.95

CITROEN
- **SM Autohistory** 90+ ill., 136 pp. . . . $14.98

COBRA
- **AC & Cobra** 350 ill., Dalton-Watson . . . $29.95
- **Racing Cobra** Christy, 208 pp., 300 ill. . . $24.95

FERRARI
- **Ferrari Legend Road Cars** Prunet 500 ill. . . . $45.00
- **Ferrari Daytona** 160 pp., 150 ill, 8 pp. color . . . $34.95
- **I Love GTO** 104 pp., 142 col. ill. . . . $19.95
- **Cplt. Guide to FE 308** by Wyss 120 ill. . . $14.95
- **Ferrari 250 GTO Autohistory** 90+ ill. . . . $14.95
- **Ferrari Berlinetta (Groh)** . . . $175.00
- **Ferrari 308 & Mondial Autohistory** . . . $14.95
- **Ferrari 4-seaters Autohistory** . . . $14.95

FIAT
- **Fiat X1/9 Autohistory** . . . $14.95

JAGUAR-SS
- **Jaguar XK** Harvey 229 ill., 23 color . . . $29.95
- **Jaguar Sports Cars** Skilletter 360 pp., 400 ill. . . . $34.95
- **History of a great Brit. Car** 179 ill. . . . $24.95
- **E Type End of an Era** Harvey 236 pp. . . $29.95
- . . .**Since 45** by Busenkell 151 pp., 144 ill. . . . $19.95
- **XK Collectors Guide** 128 pp. . . . $18.95
- **Classic Saloons Coll. Guide** by Harvey . . $18.95
- **E Type Coll. Guide** Skilletter 160 ill. . . . $18.95
- **D Type and XKSS** by Robson Autohistory . . . $14.95
- **E Type Autohistory** 136 pp. . . . $14.95
- **XJ6 Autohistory** . . . $14.95

LAMBORGHINI
- **Lamborghini** by Borel 202 ill., 130 color . . . $59.95
- **Lambo Miura** 160 pp., 150 ill. . . . $24.95
- **Lambo Collectors Guide** . . . $18.95
- **Lambo Contach. Autohistory** 136 pp. . . $14.95

LOTUS
- **Lotus Elite, Elan, Europa** 248 pp., 100 ill. . . . $29.95
- **Story of Lotus 47-60** I. Smith. . . . $20.95
- **Story of Lotus 61-71 D** Nye . . . $25.95
- **Legend of Lotus Seven** 224 pp., 150 ill. . . . $29.95
- **Elan and Europa Collectors Guide** . . . $18.95
- **Esprit Autohistory** . . . $14.95

MASERATI
- **Complete History from 1926** Orsin/Zagan . . . $59.95
- **Sports, Racing and GT** 2nd Ed. . . . $28.95
- **Bora & Merak Autohistory** . . . $14.95

MERCEDES BENZ
- **Mighty Mercedes 450 photos** . . . $27.50
- **MB 300 SL Autohistory** 136 pp. . . . $14.95
- **MB Roadsters Setright Autohistory** . . . $14.95

MG
- **Art of Abington** 256 pp, 480 ill. . . . $37.50
- **T Series MG Collectors Guide** 128 pp. . . $18.95
- **MGB Guide to purchase & restoration** . . $19.95
- **MGA Autohistory McComb** . . . $14.95
- **MGB Autohistory McComb** . . . $14.95

MINI
- **Mini Cooper & S Autohistory** 90+ ill. . . . $14.95

MORGAN
- **Moggie Purchase, Maint., Enjoyment** . . . $29.95

PANTERA
- **DeTomaso Automobiles** Wyss 208 pp., 200 ill. . . . $29.95
- **DeTomaso Pantera** by Norbye Autohistory . . . $14.95

PORSCHE
- **Excellence was expected AQ** 1000+ ill. . . . $64.95
- **Racing Porsches** Matsuda Coll. 70 color ill. . . . $52.50
- **Porsches for the Road** 250 ill., 125 color . . . $39.95
- **Porsche Book** Boschen/Barth 650 ill. . . . $29.95
- **911 Story** by Frere 2nd Ed., 143 ill. . . . $27.95
- **911 Collectors Guide** by Cotton . . . $13.95
- **Porsche Year 82** Miller 100+ ill. . . . $17.95
- **356 Autohistory** 136 pp., 90+ ill. . . . $14.95
- **911 & Turbo Autohistory** . . . $14.95

SAAB
- **SAAB Turbo** by Robson Autohistory . . . $14.95

SUNBEAM
- **Tiger, Alpine, Rapier** 175 pp., 157 ill. . . $24.95

TRIUMPH
- **TR 2 & TR 3 Parts Catalog** 374 pp., 153 ill. . . . $30.00
- **TR Spitfire** Robson, 192 pp., 200 ill. . . . $19.95
- **Triumph TRs Collectors Guide** Robson . . $18.95

TVR
- **Success against the ods** . . . $18.95
- **TVR Collectors Guide** . . . $18.95

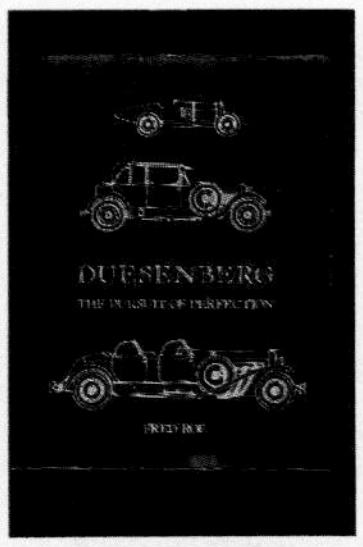

DUESENBERG–The pursuit of perfection by Fred Roe. This wonderful Dalton-Watson book illustrates and details nearly every Duesenberg ever produced. High quality production. Winner of the Thomas McKean Memorial Cup, 1982. Hb, 8″×10″, 288 pp, 550 ill. incl. interiors, engines, early racers, 1 color plate **$59.95**

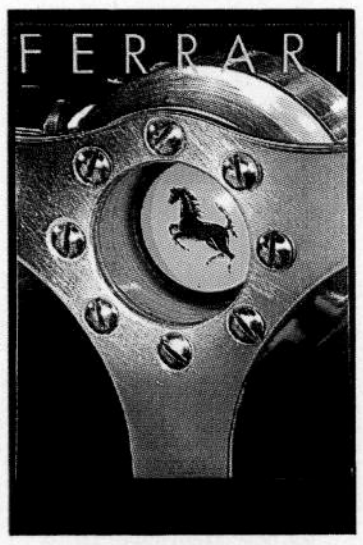

THE 1984 FERRARI CALENDAR (cover shown: 1983). As before, this is the most impressive motoring calendar published. It contains 12 superlarge Ferrari shots of the highest quality. A definite collectors item **$39.95**
Still available: Ferrari Calendar 1983, **$39.95**; Ferrari Calendar 1982, **$39.95**; all three, **$100.00.**

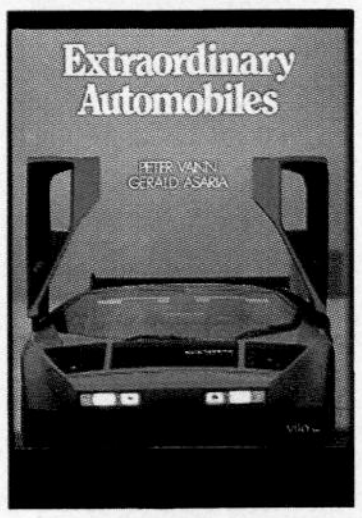

EXTRAORDINARY AUTOMOBILES by P. Vann and G. Asania. An incredible color book showing the world's most extraordinary and exotic cars of recent years–a real must for the enthusiast–there is simply no better compilation on the subject. Hb, 9¼″×11¾″, 224 pp, 205 color ill., 34 two-page photos **$39.95**

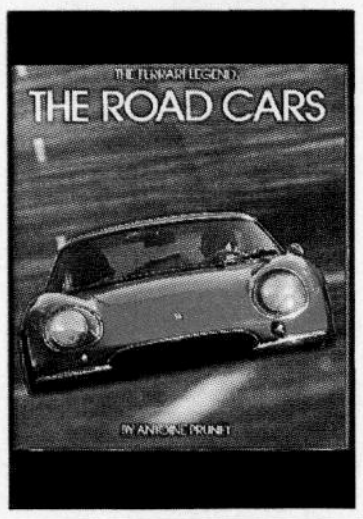

THE FERRARI LEGEND: THE ROAD CARS by Antoine Prunet. From the TIPO 125 Sport of 1946 to the 308, Ferrari have made more high performance cars–over 500 varieties–than any other marque. This lavish volume in the Ferrari Legend series examines all the road cars in detail. Hb, 8½″×10″, 446 pp, 500 ill., 97 in color **$45.00**

MAIL ORDER

SEND TO: ALBION SCOTT
Dept. CA, 48 East 50th Street, N.Y., NY 10022

Name [illegible] Date [illegible]
Address [illegible] BOX 237
State [illegible] Postcode Zip [illegible]

Please send the books listed below

QTY.	TITLE	PRICED EACH	
	6737007	599	5
	980-19289	399	5
	5955249	450	0
	760	599	5
		149	5
		149	5
		799	5
		673	10

Enclosed is my ☑ Check
☑ Money Order (Do not send cash)
Charge to my ☐ Master Card ☐ Visa
☐ American Express
Card Holder ____
Card No. ____
Good Through ____
☑ Do not ship UPS

Total Amount of Merchandise		
Deduct 10% if over $150		
Subtotal		
NY Residents add Sales Tax		
Handling Fee Foreign	3 4	00 00
FINAL TOTAL		

PLEASE NOTE: Prices ruling at time of dispatch

To order by mail—Send orders accompanied by remittance. Checks and postal orders must be made payable to: Motobooks. Postage & packaging US: $3.00. orders. Overseas $4.00 all orders (surface mail only). Telephone and mail orders accepted on VISA/Mastercharge and American Express (212) 980-1928.

☐ PLEASE SEND YOUR CATALOG
Dealer inquiries invited
1-800-654-6505

WHERE YOU CAN BUY

NEW YORK
ALBION SCOTT MOTOBOOKS
48 E. 50TH ST. 3RD. FLOOR
NEW YORK, NY 10022
Mon - Fri 10 - 7, Sat 10 - 6
(212) 980-1928/9

FLORIDA
BOOKSHOP OF KENDALL MALL
8865 SW 107 AVENUE
MIAMI, FLA 33176
Mon - Fri 9 - 9, Sun 9 - 5
(305) 595-5249

CALIFORNIA
CLASSIC BOOK AND MODEL
3800 EAST COAST HIGHWAY
CORONA DEL MAR, CA 92625
Tues - Sat 11 - 5
(714) 673-7007

MOTOBOOKS

EXCLUSIVE, HARD-TO-FIND MOTORBOOKS

1940 Mercury Town Sedan

Ford Motor Company entered the medium-priced field for the first time with introduction of the Mercury in late 1938. Mainly the inspiration of Henry Ford's only son Edsel, the new make was conceived as a "super deluxe" Ford to fill the big price gap that had long existed in the firm's product line. Styled by Bob Gregorie, the first-year 1939 models looked much like that year's Fords but rode a four-inch longer wheelbase (116 inches), were somewhat heavier, and used an enlarged version of the familiar Ford flathead V-8 producing 95 instead of 85 bhp. Offered in four

body styles, Mercury proved a hit in its inaugural year and would go on to be a mainstay at Ford Motor Company.

Our feature car is one of the follow-up 1940 models, which were much the same as the '39s aside from a minor but effective facelift done in the manner of the ever-popular 1940 Fords. This Town Sedan carried an original list price of $987, and was one of 81,128 Mercurys built for the model year. The rarest and most expensive of the 1940 models was the new convertible sedan, priced at $1212. Only 1000 or so were produced.

Owner Dan Darling of Elgin, Illinois, found this car in good condition in May 1982, and paid $3500

complete undercarriage steaming and painting. Though the work is not yet quite complete, this car took home nine first-place trophies in the summer of 1983, including a first prize in the Illinois Region AACA show.

Darling has no other collectibles, but he drives this one regularly during the summer and has added about 3500 miles to the car's original 62,000. Though he could easily sell it now for $10,000, he probably won't.

for it. The previous owner had resurrected it back in 1968 when he found it resting quietly in a field. Darling has invested some $3000 in it himself, mostly for cosmetic work and a

Chrysler's Town & Country 1941-1984: Rare Elegance

From Detroit's salad days before World War II came the most elegant "woodie" ever: the Chrysler Town & Country. Here's the story of these rare and desirable cars—and of their collectible 1980s successor.

by Michael Richards

In case you haven't noticed, Chrysler Corporation has been doing great things lately. The exciting new Chrysler Laser and Dodge Daytona sports coupes and the ingenious T-115 "garageable" vans lead a fleet of what have to be the most interesting—and, in their way, the most significant—Mopars in 20 or more years. The company whose survival nobody would bet on three years ago celebrates its 60th anniversary in 1984 with renewed confidence that it's going to be around for a long time to come.

Chrysler is again bringing us the same kind of integrated design and honest engineering, in the modern context, that we remember it for in its best years. And the Corporation has a memory, too: for the first time in 35 years it is offering a Town & Country convertible. What better occasion for a look back at the splendid T&Cs of the '40s, every one of them as collectible today as, no doubt, the new one will be in a couple of decades.

Pass your eyes over the plankwood behemoths on these pages. These cars were the essence of the T&C idea in the early postwar era and were utterly right for their time, possessing a class and character that made most of their contemporaries seem just plain dull. Check the woodwork: hewn of white ash, fitted and mitred with the perfection of a Hepplewhite highboy, with joints so smooth you could blindfold yourself and not be able to tell where they were. Look at the body panels: heavy, iron-like objects that fit together solidly; doors, hood, and trunklid that clunk shut like the vaults at Chase-Manhattan Bank. Inspect the brightwork: lavishly applied, every square inch finished to mirror brilliance and attached with hardly a bolt or screwhead in sight. Climb behind the wheel and take in your surroundings: a colossal radio with more steel in it than an entire Ford Pinto, able to utter deep, fat tones no transistor can duplicate; a jumbo steering wheel you can really get hold of, sprouting from a steering column as thick as a sapling; a great club of a

Left and above: Easily the most interesting addition to the '41 Chrysler lineup, the original Town & Country may well qualify as the world's first hatchback sedan. Its rear roof was sloped, not squared, and its unique "clamshell" rear doors also set it apart from contemporary wagons.

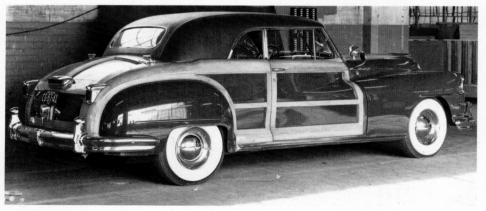

Left, top to bottom: Wraparound grille bars marked the '42 T&C, here with accessory spotlight and roof rack. Roof rack shifted to all-chrome and became standard for the T&C sedan in July 1947. A T&C hardtop was proposed for 1946, but only seven prototypes were built and only one survives today. Dave Wallace's personal T&C hardtop, here with retrofit padded roof; this is believed to be the surviving prototype. Opposite page: The eight-cylinder convertible accounted for the bulk of T&C production through 1950.

handbrake you grab at and yank to hold the car in position; acres of plastic, that rock-hard, postwar, marbelized stuff more closely related to Bakelite than to the plastics of today. In 1948 all this cost $3420, roughly $15,000 in today's money. But don't think you could build one like it now for less than $50,000—assuming you could even find craftsmen with the requisite skill to put it together.

"Such cars are not interesting because they have unique solutions to the automotive problem," wrote Ted West about a similar Chrysler 15 years ago, "but simply because they are in some way 'foreign' to more modern automobiles. The craftsmanship and general feeling of opulence of this car, for instance, clearly distinguished it from American cars of recent years." Certainly, we'll never see a car like the '48 Town & Country again.

The T&C story is familiar enough, having been chronicled over the years in just about every car publication and a half-dozen books. Most of the research avenues have long since been explored, so we can capsulize its history and with authority. The idea began in 1941, not with a flashy convertible or lavish sedan, but with a station wagon conceived by the then general manager of Chrysler Division, Dave Wallace. Chrysler had never had a wagon, and in the late 1930s, Wallace decided it needed one. But not the clumsy, boxy creations then being ladled on various chassis by traditional bodybuilders like Cantrell, Baker Raulang, Hercules, Mifflinburg and the rest. Wallace wanted a tight, streamlined wagon that looked more like a sedan. Because these suppliers of woody wagon bodywork looked on such an idea with bewilderment, Wallace turned to his own engineers, among the most formidably competent in the industry. He told them what he wanted, and he got it.

Wallace was ahead of his time with this concept, although he was not quite alone. Industrial designer Brooks Stevens had conjured up a rakish semi-wood body with a double hatchback for a 1938 Packard One Twenty, but that was strictly a custom order. Wallace was the first to bring a sedan-like wagon to mass production—if you'll concede that the thousand-odd T&Cs built each year in 1941-42 constitutes "mass production." In so doing, he anticipated the sedan-based wagon, that darling of suburbia in the Fifties and Sixties, by a good 10 to 15 years.

Wallace's body engineers succeeded brilliantly. In place of the typical, rattling, awkward-looking wood structure with separate liftgate and tailgate they conjured up a smooth, fastback-style four-door featuring double "clamshell" doors hinged at the sides. These opened to expose an enormous cargo bay, and didn't prang anybody's knees in the process. The

interior held two or three large bench seats, thus offering six- or nine-passenger capacity. The body was placed on the 121.5-inch-wheelbase C-28W Windsor chassis with the 112-bhp L-head six and standard Fluid Drive and "Vacumatic" transmission.

T&C historian Don Narus has pointed out (see sidebar) that Chrysler had to "learn" to build the T&C, largely because Briggs, the firm's regular body supplier, had no such experience. Briggs was primarily a metal-working company, and did produce the T&C's cowl and floorpan, front

Town & Country: Origins of the Name

Most researchers have credited the Town & Country name to Paul Hafer of the Boyertown [Pennsylvania] Body Works. This firm had submitted several designs for woody wagon bodies to Chrysler in an attempt to obtain some work. Hafer, who sketched these proposals for Dodge Division in 1939, used "Town & Country" along with "Country Gentleman" and "Country Club Sport" in his drawings. Dodge, of course, never built a Town & Country, though it appears likely that Hafer's title was picked up by Chrysler Division.

Even so, that's not the only possibility. The name had been used once before by another, non-Chrysler make, and several enthusiasts have stated that it appeared in an Airflow brochure. Whatever its origins, it's perfect, a name that implies casual elegance and easy sophistication. And with the revivial of the concept for 1984, it is now one of the longest-lived titles in industry history.

Building the T&C Convertible

Although Chrysler had plenty of experience building its prewar Town & Country wagons, it had to learn anew about building convertibles for the 1946-48 T&C. The ragtop's structure was entirely different from that of other Chrysler models, of course, and there was the added problem of no steel top to provide the desired torsional strength.

After considerable trial and error, engineers devised a conventional cowl and floor section for the woody convertible, with a surrounding steel beltline and the rear fenders tied together by a steel shelf. The B-pillars were wood, supported at their bases by tunnels that stretched across the floorpan to meet upright angle iron supports. Sheetmetal carried the winding mechanisms for the rear side windows, which helped remove stress from the wood rear-quarter body areas. The doors were mainly solid wood, too, and because of their weight, a sheetmetal leading edge was attached to support their hinges. As in the rear quarters, sheetmetal housed the window regulators.

This complex construction did not lend itself to conveyor-type assembly methods, and extensive use of welding machines was out of the question. Accordingly, the metal components were filed and welded by hand, and wood subassemblies were each put together by one or two workers using crafts more appropriate for a boatyard than a car plant. Ply-metal panels were installed in the ash framing by means of a hammer, wedges, glue, and rope caulk. Teams moved from one body to the next, each handling a specific task. To say the Town & Country involved a lot of time-consuming hand labor is an understatement. For example, it took 12 workers just to install each convertible top. Once the body was completed, it was mated to its chassis in the usual manner. Assembly then proceeded from station to station, much like that of the conventional models.

Compared to the normal production-line cars, T&Cs moved at a snail's pace, which accounts for both their low volume and high price. Production from 1946 through 1948 averaged only 10 units per day, and it took fully three eight-hour shifts to achieve that. But the slow going produced amazing results, and materials were the very best. The white ash, for example, was not only more durable than most woods but was also unequalled for the beauty of its grain, which contrasted perfectly with the mahogany insert panels. Also, the framework was not made of a single piece of wood, so it was possible to match grain patterns exactly. The individual pieces were carefully selected and matched, and were then laminated into the larger sections that made up the entire framework. It all added to the cost, but you couldn't find a more carefully or better built car for the money than the classic Town & Country. *by Don Narus*

end, and steel roof. But the rest was Chrysler's. Wallace had picked an outside firm, Pekin Wood Products of Helena, Arkansas, to supply the white ash body framing. (Conjecture has it that Wallace, who also happened to be Pekin's president, devised the T&C just to help keep that company in business.) The inner panels were initially made of Honduran mahogany. In 1947, Chrysler switched to Di-Noc decals for the inserts as an economy move, though we should note these were so realistic that it was nearly impossible to distinguish them from real mahogany.

Wallace earmarked a section of Chrysler's Jefferson Avenue plant in Detroit for T&C assembly. Required jigs and fixtures were installed and a small force of craftsmen was trained to build the body, weld the steel roof to the steel cowl, and mate wood to metal with angle irons and steel butt plates. Production was 997 units for 1941, all but 200 being nine-passenger models, followed by 999 of the 1942s.

Wright

During this period there were also two eight-cylinder T&C prototypes built on the 127.5-inch-wheelbase New Yorker chassis. The only major changes for '42 involved hidden running boards (via extended lower door panels) and a front-end facelift with the grillework extended around to the edges of the front fenders. Because of its late introduction, the Town & Country was one of the few '42 models produced in higher quantity than in '41 despite the early shutdown of all car production in February 1942 because of the war effort.

Although T&Cs were the strongest wagons ever produced up to that time, thanks mainly to the sturdy all-steel roof without the customary fabric insert, Chrysler product planners decided that utility wasn't really what sold them. What mattered was their unusual and handsome looks, a beautiful blend of woodwork and metal. Besides, Chrysler was planning its first all-steel station wagons even before the war ended (Plymouth broke

the ice in that field in 1949). So, Wallace altered his game plan once car production resumed in 1946. Now there would be a distinct line of wood-trimmed luxury models bearing the Town & Country name, including a formal-roof brougham sedan, a convertible, a conventional sedan, a two-seat roadster, even a pillarless two-door coupe.

The last was arguably the most interesting and significant Town & Country. It was the first modern hardtop, three years ahead of GM's pioneering pillarless trio and grandaddy of the body style that would dominate the American auto industry for the next 20 years. Chrysler built it by grafting the steel roof from its club coupe onto a conventional T&C convertible, but had second thoughts about volume production. Only seven were completed, and only one of these survives today.

Also announced for 1946 were the brougham, a roadster with huge blind quarters (which prefigured the later

The Town & Country convertible for 1948. The structural wood certainly added welcome relief to the bulbous Chrysler styling, but by the time this car was built the company had switched from all-wood panels to Di-Noc decal inserts. However, they were very difficult to distinguish from the genuine mahogany panels used earlier. The white ash framing was used through the 1946-48 production run.

Dodge Wayfarer), and a six-cylinder convertible on the shorter wheelbase. However, except for a single brougham and short-chassis convertible, both prototypes, none of these saw actual production. "The sales department was just fishing around in the beginning," remembered stylist Buzz Grisinger. "Postwar plans were pretty much a hurry-up thing. There weren't any clay models or production prototypes...We just designed a series of different styles and brushed on wood trim where we thought it looked aesthetically best. Sales took it from there."

25

And where the sales department took it was to convertibles and four-door sedans. More than half of the 16,000 T&Cs built through 1950 were the 1946-48 convertibles. All employed the holdover 127.5-inch-wheelbase chassis, designated C-39, and were powered by the New Yorker's familiar 135-bhp L-head straight eight. Priced $600 above the standard New Yorker soft-top, these were the cars prized by many Hollywood heavies. For example, Leo Carillo, perhaps best remembered now for his television role as the Cisco Kid's sidekick Pancho, liked his T&C convertible so much that he fitted it with the head of a longhorn steer—its eyes wired to blink along with the turn signals—and monogrammed hubcaps. This car later became part of the Harrah Collection in Reno, Nevada.

The 1946-48 Town & Country convertible was so all-fired glamorous that it tends to eclipse the 121.5-inch-wheelbase four-door sedans, which in their own way were just as stunning. Their interiors were richly finished with wood paneling set off by leather, Bedford cord, Saran plastic, or vinyl upholstery, plus color-keyed carpeting. A lovely wood luggage rack was optional (its roof runners were changed to chrome-plated metal in mid-1947, when it was made standard). To many collectors, the sedans are the real sleepers among the early postwar T&Cs because they're a lot scarcer than the ragtops. Only 224 sedans were designated 1946 models, 2651 were '47s, 1175 were '48s. A mere 100 of the '46s were eight-cylinder models on the longer New Yorker wheelbase, the rarest production Town & Country of all.

When most Detroit manufacturers launched their first all-new designs for 1949, the Town & Country began to wane. It had, after all, been only a stop-gap item with little sales significance. Its greatest benefit in the immediate postwar period was to entice people back into Chrysler showrooms—people who would, it was hoped, be inspired to order one of the more conventional, less costly models. Like the contemporary Ford and Mercury Sportsman convertibles and the Nash Suburban sedan, the T&C was a marketing concept designed to add needed glamour to a line of 1946-48 cars that were little more than warmed-over '42s.

Opposite page: A full line of Town & Country models including sedans and a pillarless hardtop were planned for 1949, when Chrysler introduced its first all-new postwar designs. However, only a convertible emerged. Wood trim was now more decorative than functional as it had been previously, but at least it contrived to give the cars a distinctive appearance, especially from the rear. Above: The promised T&C hardtop arrived for 1950—but then the convertible was dropped. Ad copy is amazingly prophetic. Only about 700 Town & Country Newports were constructed, versus some 1000 of the '49 soft-top models. Below: Like lesser versions of K.T. Keller's "boxy" new postwar generation, the 1950 Town & Country Newport offered vast interior space front and rear.

The Town & Country Newport hardtop coupe for 1950 was the last of the glamorous wood-body models. Owner: Dan Hrishko. Opposite page: The T&C tradition continues today with this convertible based on the front-drive LeBaron series. Wood trim is entirely imitation.

Like other early postwar woodies, the Town & Country was primarily a marketing concept designed to add much-needed glamour to a line of 1946-48 cars that were little more than warmed-over '42s.

Thus, it was no surprise that when Chrysler trotted out its all-new body design for 1949, T&C offerings were trimmed. Only an eight-cylinder convertible with considerably less woodwork was available, and sales for the model totalled exactly 1000. The model returned with the same basic body for 1950 but as a Newport hardtop (a convertible was considered but scratched). Like the '49, it was mounted on the 131.5-inch New Yorker chassis and was powered by the familiar 135-bhp 323.5-cid straight eight. Unique to the '50 T&C (and the long-wheelbase Imperial) were disc brakes, one of the first applications on a U.S. production automobile.

The name was too good to lose, of course, and Chrysler never gave it up. Along with the T&C Newport for 1950 appeared two Town & Country station wagons, either wood or steel, in the bottom-line Royal series. The hardtop vanished the following year, but the wagons were expanded with

entries in the three lower lines, Windsor, Saratoga and New Yorker. From here on, whenever Chrysler had a wagon to sell it would be called Town & Country. But wood, as a decorative or support structure, vanished after 1950, and what looked like wood was merely decal.

During model year 1968 the original Town & Country concept, in spirit at least, made a temporary return. In time for the mid-year selling season there arrived a new option called "Sportsgrain." It was available for convertibles and two-door hardtops in the Newport series, then Chrysler's bread-and-butter line, priced in the competitive $3300-4500 range and available in six body styles including two Town & Country wagons. To avoid confusion, cars so equipped did not wear the Town & Country badge, and some enthusiasts were undoubtedly thankful for that. Indeed, the Sportsgrain Newport can be accurately summed up as the standard car

Wright

Left: Though not the rarest production T&C, the 1949 convertible is the scarcest of the volume ragtops and an eminently collectible automobile. Right: Introduced mid-way through the 1983 model year, the front-drive LeBaron Town & Country convertible sports several improvements for 1984, including a more spacious rear seat area.

with $126 worth of simulated-wood paneling plastered to the bodysides as on the wagon. It didn't look bad, but it didn't knock your eyes out either. And as a successor to the real Town & Country it was a non-starter. Sales were 965 hardtops and 175 convertibles—which explains why Sportsgrain disappeared for good after this one year.

Suddenly it's 1984, and the Town & Country is back, this time for real. It comes to us in the LeBaron series, another long-standing Chrysler nameplate that originated in the coachbuilding days of Ray Dietrich and Tom Hibbard. LeBaron and Town & Country: it's a plush combination. Though there's no real tree wood in it, this newest T&C is nevertheless a first-rate reincarnation of the spirit and style of the original.

Actually, there are two LeBaron T&Cs, a five-door wagon and a convertible. The ragtop has naturally been getting the most attention from both the press and buyers. And why not? It's not only one of the few domestic convertibles you can buy new these days, it's also one of the best. And, as the first open-air Town &

Country in almost two generations, it's the model that most strongly evokes memories of the great late-1940s classics.

As most car watchers know, Chrysler has used the LeBaron nameplate for the past quarter century. It has graced a variety of models ranging from the outsized Imperials of the early '60s to upmarket derivatives of the firm's late-'70s mid-size cars. The current LeBaron was introduced for 1982 as a plusher, classier-looking rendition of the practical front-wheel-drive K-body compacts that debuted the previous year. The Town & Country name was revived at mid-model year. Though the wagon was expected, a convertible was not—let alone one cast in the image of one of Chrysler's most memorable cars. But it was all part of the plan to put more pizzazz and competitiveness into the company's offerings, and Chrysler's miracle worker, Lee A. Iacocca, has never been one for doing the predictable.

Ordinarily, the simple addition of wood-like appliques to an otherwise standard production car wouldn't be enough to garner more than a stifled yawn from enthusiasts. But there's

something different about the LeBaron Town & Country convertible. Call it character, call it nostalgia, this car is *noticed*, attracting as much interest as some performance machines and far more than its non-woody linemates.

Like all LeBarons, the new convertible rides a 100.3-inch wheelbase and is just shy of 15 feet in overall length, making it the shortest T&C in history as well as the lightest. It's also obviously the first with front-wheel drive. But it is not unlike its massive forbearers when it comes to smooth performance, fine ride, and quietness at cruising speeds. And it offers something no T&C has ever had before: roadability. Standard equipment includes the 2.6-liter (156-cid) Mitsubishi-built four-cylinder engine that's optional for other models, teamed with Chrysler's still-excellent three-speed TorqueFlite automatic. A more exciting prospect—and an item definitely suited to the convertible's sporty nature—is the newly optional turbocharged version of Chrysler's 2.2-liter (135-cid) overhead-cam "Trans-4" engine with electronic port fuel injection. Scheduled for mid-year introduction, it makes this the first T&C that can truthfully be described as "fun to drive."

Other features of the '84 include more rear seat room than in the initial 1983 convertible; roll-down rear quarter windows, another improvement; a backlight made of glass instead of plastic; and more convenient roof and latch mechanisms. Preserving its luxury link with the past, the new T&C is offered with an optional Mark Cross interior package featuring genuine leather upholstery. And despite all this talk of tradition, this is a very modern car, with such high-technology attractions as computer-aided body design and a fascinating, extra-cost electronic instrument cluster.

The LeBaron T&C convertible is available in three pearlescent shades—Mink brown, Gunmetal blue, and Garnet red, which is in

keeping with traditional T&C convertible colors. Is the '84 as collectible an automobile as its classic predecessors? Probably not, at least not for a good many years yet, but we wouldn't discourage you from considering one on that basis. If nothing else, the revival of this car indicates the T&C heritage still matters at Highland Park, even as Chrysler campaigns for an increased share of the market in the highly competitive Eighties. And, by the way, they're probably going to get it.

A replica of the original? No, nothing like that. But the 1984 Town & Country is also more than mere transportation. Like the original, it's a handsome convertible with a difference: stylish and plush, indefinably yet unmistakably classy. Back in the Forties, you know, Chrysler was the number-two American automaker. With cars like this it's not inconceivable they could soon be in that spot again. Think we're kidding? It would only take a shift of three or four percentage points to do it. As we said, Chrysler has been doing some great things lately.

Town & Country Production

1941
9-passenger wagon, 6 cyl, 121.5" wb	797
6-passenger wagon, 6 cyl, 121.5" wb	200
9-passenger wagon, 8 cyl, 127.5" wb	1*

1942
9-passenger wagon, 6 cyl, 121.5" wb	849
6-passenger wagon, 6 cyl, 121.5" wb	150
9-passenger wagon, 8 cyl, 127.5" wb	1*

1946
2d convertible, 8 cyl, 127.5" wb	1935
4d sedan, 8 cyl, 127.5" wb	100
4d sedan, 6 cyl, 121.5" wb	124
2d hardtop, 8 cyl, 127.5" wb	7*
2d brougham, 6 cyl, 121.5" wb	1*
2d convertible, 6 cyl, 121.5" wb	1*

*prototypes

1947
2d convertible, 8 cyl, 127.5" wb	3136
4d sedan, 6 cyl, 121.5" wb	2651

1948
2d convertible, 8 cyl, 127.5" wb	3309
4d sedan, 6 cyl, 121.5" wb	1175

1949
2d convertible, 8 cyl, 131.5" wb	1000

1950
2d Newport hardtop, 8 cyl, 131.5" wb	700
4d Royal wagon, 6 cyl, 125.5" wb, wood	599
4d Royal wagon, 6 cyl, 125.5" wb, steel	100

1951-1983
Name applied to wagons in all Chrysler series when wagons offered.

1968 "Sportsgrain"
2d Newport hardtop, 8 cyl, 124" wb	965
2d Newport convertible, 8 cyl, 124" wb	175

Avanti: Forward, Backward, Forward

It's had more ups and downs than a sine curve,
but the Avanti is a survivor. And the '84 is the best one yet.

by Richard M. Langworth

Few cars in current production can trace their design origins back 20-odd years. Those that can, like the Jaguar XJ sedan and the Porsche 911, have lasted as long as they have because they represent a pinnacle of sorts. Their manufacturers simply haven't devised anything to replace them that would be either more exciting or better. Different maybe, but not necessarily better. Only one such American car comes to mind in this context and that's the Avanti, nee Avanti II, nee Studebaker Avanti. Like the 911, it remains unabashedly a product of its time; it ceased to be a state-of-the-art car long ago. But nobody's complaining. The Avanti was so "right" to begin with that even its parentage—and the death of that par-

ent—has failed to condemn it to history. When its maker departed ignominiously from the ranks of U.S. car manufacturers, the Avanti's friends moved in to keep it alive. In fact, it's just happened again.

The story begins over 20 years ago with the arrival of Sherwood Harry Egbert as president of Studebaker Corporation. A hard-driving manager fresh from success as president of McCulloch in California, he was determined to save the ailing South Bend company, and saw a fleet of modern, exciting cars as the way to do it. Egbert knew the secret of such cars was able design talent, and he went about hiring it. As an interim measure he signed on Brooks Stevens to dramatically update the aging Hawk

coupe and freshen up the dowdy Lark. Then he approached Raymond Loewy with an idea for a ground-up *gran turismo* that would spawn an entirely new generation of Studebakers on the leading edge of automotive design.

Loewy and company had been involved with Studebaker since the late Thirties. They created the vital, low-price Champion for 1939, the all-new

Above: The 1984 Avanti will be as collectible in the future as the original Studebaker models and Avanti IIs are now. Shown is one of the first 50 specially equipped production examples. Opposite page: Rectangular headlamp bezels were a feature of the '64 Studebaker Avanti, but not all cars had them. This meticulously maintained specimen belongs to Avanti enthusiast Tom Griffith.

Far left: Mrs. Viola Loewy poses with her husband's Loewy-BMW exercise in 1957. It was built by Pinchon-Parat of Paris, which would later build the Avanti-based sedan mockups at Studebaker. Near left: The Lancia "Loraymo" from 1960 was a further evolution of the designer's sports car ideas, many of which would resurface in the Avanti. Upper left: The 1963 Avanti. Owner: Ken Stiles.

1947 "head start" models, and the matchless Starliner/Starlight coupes of 1953. Loewy's last job for South Bend had been the 1956 Hawk. Egbert phoned him in January 1961, a few weeks before Egbert was due to start work. Would Loewy consider renewing his consultancy? Loewy said he might, if he had a free hand. On February 2nd, he sent Egbert several documents relating to his earlier Studebaker efforts, "a few clippings and photographs which you may find interesting." It was the beginning of the Avanti project.

On March 9th, Loewy received another call from Egbert. "He wanted to talk to me about a new sports car," the designer remembered. "He said, 'Raymond, I want you to do it at once...and it must be an absolute knockout. The finished clay model must be done in six weeks. Can you do it?' I said I could, 'providing you let me do it the way I want and give me complete freedom of action...I want to work it out in Palm Springs where I have my winter home...free from interference, and especially free from well-meant suggestions.'" Egbert agreed.

"I had decided on a design concept almost immediately after Egbert's first communication," Loewy recalled. "It was an evolution of my thinking in three earlier experimental cars, the Lancia Loraymo, the Loewy BMW and Loewy Jaguar. All three featured large, convex backlights uninterrupted by a pillar, and the Loraymo exhibited a fuselage similar to what I had in mind, a 'coke-bottle' shape in plan view, designed for optimum aerodynamics."

Loewy now secured the services of three top aides. Robert F. Andrews had worked with chief stylist Frank Spring at Hudson and with Loewy on the Studebaker account in the 1950s. Tom Kellogg was a young sketch artist known for his ability to translate imaginative ideas to paper. John Ebstein was a vice-president of the Loewy-Snaith industrial design firm

in New York City. That Loewy was able to put together such a stellar group within a week says much about him and his organizational ability.

The team was spirited away to Loewy's small ranch house in the desert outside Palm Springs, where they must have felt like characters in a James Bond thriller. "We had no idea what was up, except that it was terribly secret and a rush project," Bob Andrews remembered. "R. L. closed us up tight...He disconnected the telephone, stopped all the clocks and banned wives and girl friends. We worked 16 hours a day for weeks. It was so grueling that I took to fooling around. I'd walk up behind Tom, making loud heel clicks in imitation of the boss. He'd drop his butt or coffee and bend down over the drafting board, and I'd whisper obscenities in his ears. It was the tomfoolery that kept us all from going balmy."

Before his crew arrived, Loewy had tacked large sheets of paper to the walls, establishing his general theme. Some of the legends read: "Coke-shape a must"; "Wedgy silhouette"; "Off-center gunsight panel on hood"; "Use scoop—no grille." A stout rollbar was designed into the roofline, cleverly hidden from the outside and well padded.

The front end progressed from conventional bumper/grille combinations to a smooth, sharply drooping wedge with an air intake underneath. One early small scale model did contain modest grillework on the "face" of the wedge, "like a receding hairline." Loewy rejoiced when Eugene Hardig, Studebaker chief engineer, advised that it wouldn't be necessary because he had devised a new radiator.

The rear end, an upswept ducktail with wrapped taillights and a thin-section bumper, was implicit in most early sketches, and changed only in detail on the way to the production Avanti. Likewise the coke-bottle fuselage, though much revision was made to the wheelarch "re-entry" curves so that they would resemble the trajectories of objects reentering Earth's atmosphere from space, reflecting Loewy's recent experience as a consultant to NASA. The openings were flared at the tops in the first scale model, but the bulges were ultimately deleted. "From the rear view they provided visual stability and I think

Only a week after it began work, the Avanti design team had produced its first scale model. Barely five weeks after the project began, the full-size clay was complete.

Below: One of the first small-scale clay models was considerably revised later on. Bottom: The 1/8th-scale clay taken by Loewy to South Bend. "Receeding hairline" grille, quad headlamps, sloped front fenders and flared wheel arches were all omitted.

they looked good," Loewy said. "At the time we felt they interfered with our prime directive, which was purity of line. We felt they weren't necessary."

The asymmetrical hump on the hood stemmed from Loewy's BMW and Loraymo exercises. "It was exactly in the axis of the steering wheel column, and straight," Loewy said. "If you were on a straight highway, that panel was oriented forward where the roadway would blend with the horizon, parallel to the centerline of the chassis frame. It made car and driver integral, like the gunsight of a gun." It also oriented vision downward: Loewy induced a noticeable front-end rake to the Avanti that contributed to its aggressive, hungry, ground-hugging appearance.

Loewy convinced Egbert the car should seat four people, not two—better for sales that way. He had a

major fight with Egbert over sunvisors, which Sherwood didn't want at all because of his height, well over six feet. They ended up compromising, with the result that Avanti sunvisors have always been skimpy.

The Avanti interior was notable for the aircraft-inspired overhead positioning of the light controls, above the windshield header, and using rocker-type switches from the lowly Lark. The functional reason for this arrangement was Loewy's desire for a clean, "safe" dashboard as free of protrusions as possible. Other knobs were grouped with a full set of engine instruments in a three-plane cluster ahead of the driver. A center console carried the heating and ventilation controls, which were chrome toggles much like those of early-'50s Mercurys, while the radio was inset into the dashboard above. Instrument lighting was red, a color Egbert had chosen as easy to read and glare-free. It also fit the general aircraft influence selected as a major design theme.

Only a week after it began work, the team produced the first ⅛-scale clay—actually a half model placed against a mirror for full effect. Aside from a slight revision to the hoodline, this shape was approved almost in its entirety. Loewy flew it to South Bend on April 2nd, by which time the engineers had laid out a full-size clay buck and stylists Randy Faurot and Bob Doehler were ready to take on the job of modeling a full-size clay.

First known as the Q or X model, the car had been christened Avanti— Italian for "forward"—by May. The name was suggested by the D'Arcy MacManus ad agency, but Egbert considered a number of others including "Packard" and "Pierce Arrow," which were rejected as anachronistic. However, Loewy did retain a Thirties flavor with the Avanti nameplate, which incorporated an arrow running through the lettering in the style of his 1932 Hupmobile logo.

There was no time or money to design a new chassis, and the best one available was the heavily reinforced Lark convertible frame with a 109-inch wheelbase. This proved too short in front and too long in back. Ebstein lengthened the rear body, but the chassis still extended a bit too far, disrupting the tucked-under look and necessitating the use of little boxes in the pan for the spring shackles. The

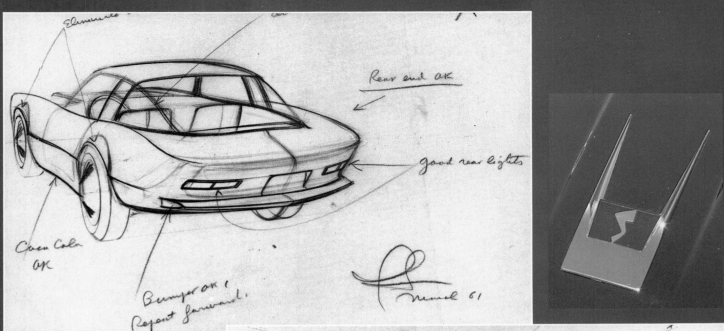

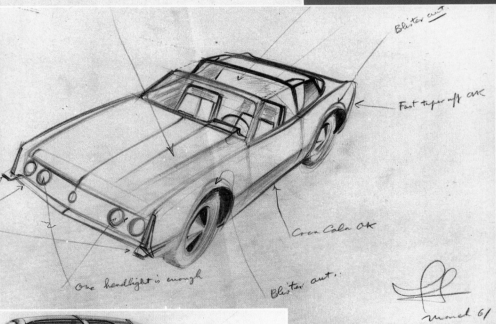

Above: An early Avanti sketch at Palm Springs, complete with Loewy's notes, shows the beautifully upswept tail, wrapped taillamps, and thin-section bumper initially contemplated. Toronado-like flared wheel openings were pondered and ultimately rejected. Right: A bit further along, with the C-pillar shape and asymmetrical hood blister used in production. After the South Bend preview, Loewy ordered his team to close up the open roof, square off the front fender leading edges, and go to single headlamps. Below: Thinner B-pillar rollbar and a Targa-style removable roof panel were considered as well; costs precluded the latter. Basic greenhouse configuration is more or less final in this sketch. Inset, above right: Matching Loewy's Avanti script was this stylized Studebaker "S" carried on the hood blister of production 1963-64 cars.

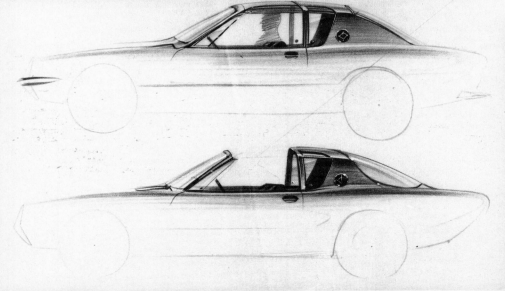

original front end was considered short by management, not by Loewy, but management prevailed and the front fenders were extended.

Only detail changes were needed as the full-size clay took shape. Egbert conked his head getting into the seating buck, and insisted that the windshield rake be less extreme; Bob Doehler came up with some extra stampings and paint that gave the old 1953 Studebaker wheel cover the effect of an alloy wheel but with none of the expense. The taillamp-backup lights were split at the trunk opening; the proposed vertical spring-back bumpers were replaced by horizontal units and front bumpers were extended around the sides; and the leading edges of the front fenders were squared off to contain the parking lamps.

By April 27, 1961, barely five weeks after the project began, the full-size clay was complete and body templates were being taken. Bob Doehler

was now attending to interior design, working with Kellogg's renderings. Cost considerations eliminated the proposed vacuum-formed Royalite interior panels and a single full-length armrest running front to rear on each side, bisected by the doors. Product planners considered the open space behind the rear seat unattractive, so a fiberboard panel was laid horizontally and given an access door to allow longer-armed passengers to dip into the trunk. Milt Antonick created the simple, two-spoke steering wheel (with a horn bar in each spoke), while Bob Doehler shaped the seats along the lines of those in the Alfa Romeo Giulietta. The gas tank filler pipe intruded into the rear cockpit due to its high position on the C-pillar, but Andrews said they decided to leave it there, covered with vinyl, "because it looked very aircraft." Most of the interior was locked up by September.

Egbert elected to use glass-reinforced plastic (GRP) for the Avanti

Considering how quickly it was created, the Avanti design has aged remarkably well. Shown is the 1963 edition. Studebaker's 289 V-8 was old but reliable, and gave quite good performance in supercharged form.

body to expedite production, against the judgment of Loewy and several production engineers. However, instead of manufacturing the body at South Bend, he was persuaded to farm out the job to Molded Fiberglass Products in Ashtabula, Ohio, which already had considerable experience with GRP as body supplier to Chevrolet for the Corvette.

Gene Hardig worked considerable magic on the old Lark convertible frame. New sway bars were installed front and rear, and rear radius rods were adopted. The gas tank was located ahead of the trunk wall, behind the rear seat, where it was well protected in the event of a collision. Other safety-oriented features included cone-type door locks from

Daimler-Benz, caliper disc brakes built by Bendix under license from Dunlop, and the integral rollbar, which also helped stiffen the body. The caliper discs were the first of their kind on an American production car and only the third application of disc brakes in postwar U.S. automotive history. Independent rear suspension with inboard discs was considered, but costs again interfered and Studebaker settled for a conventional beam axle with finned drums. Interestingly, the new management at Avanti Motors is now "prototyping" a backbone-type chassis with all-independent suspension and four-wheel discs. Good ideas never die.

The only engine Studebaker had for such a high-performance car was its old 289 V-8, and what Hardig and his engineers accomplished with it was remarkable. The standard R1 "Jet-Thrust" unit was given a ¾-race cam, heavy-duty valves and crankshaft bearings, dual-breaker distributor,

viscous fan drive, four-barrel carb and dual exhausts. Scoffers claim Egbert specified the loudest possible mufflers for his hell-bent trips to and from the plant, but Studebaker said they made for less back pressure and longer life. They certainly fitted the concept of the car. Studebaker refused to announce the R1's horsepower, but estimates put it at about 240 bhp gross.

Andy Granatelli's Paxton Products outfit provided a supercharger for a step-up version, the R2, which developed between 285 and 290 bhp. But Granatelli didn't stop here. He developed three even more potent 304.5-cid derivatives, the R3, R4, and R5. Only the R3 saw production— and then on only nine 1964 Avantis— though all save the R5 were cataloged as options throughout the entire '64 Studebaker lineup. The R3 had 9.6:1 compression with headers (later offered as R1/R2 options) and developed at least 335 bhp. The experimental,

unblown R4 used twin four-barrel carbs and had an astonishing 12:1 compression, good for 280 bhp. The very experimental R5 got a special cam grind to Paxton specs, plus magneto ignition, twin blowers (one for each cylinder bank), a Bendix fuel injection system initially developed for the V-8 Novi Indianapolis engine, and dry-sump lubrication with oil reservoir and cooler. Redlined at 7000 rpm, the R5 reportedly developed about 575 horsepower.

Though not strictly production until '64, the R3 was the engine powering the Avanti that Granatelli drove to break 29 stock car speed records at Bonneville in early 1962. He was faster than anyone had been in an American stock car under officially timed conditions. His best performance came in the flying kilometer, 168.24 mph. Streamlining was important here, although Loewy never had the benefit of a wind tunnel. The Avanti's drag coefficient was estimated in the high 0.30s at a time when most stock American cars were in the 0.50s, which suggests how effective the designing team's ideas in this area really were.

This would not be the Avanti's only appearance at Bonneville. To announce the 1964 models, Egbert sent a dozen different Studebakers— everything from a Commander six to an R5 Avanti—to the Salt Flats in October 1963. Here, Egbert himself managed 168 mph for his personal flying mile, while Bill Burke set an E-Supercharged class record in a Paxton-blown 259-cid Avanti with Weber cam, oversize valves and Schiefer clutch/flywheel. Old man Granatelli came back with his R3 to score 170.78 mph, and broke five other Class C marks in the process. Altogether, these 12 cars smashed 72 different USAC records in six classes.

But let's not forget what the stock Avanti could do. Most road tests of the basic R1 models listed 0-60 mph times of about 10.5 seconds, the standing-start quarter-mile in 17.5 seconds at about 80 mph, and top speeds of 115-120 mph. Road & Track magazine's R2 car with 4.09:1 final drive did 117 mph flat out and 0-60 mph in 7.3 seconds. The editors called this "a car for the driving sport (as opposed to the sporting driver)," but praised its good handling, first-rate brakes and "absolutely the best seats

In retrospect, the Avanti's main handicap was that it was a Studebaker, the product of a company caught in an inexorable downward spiral of public confidence. Had it been a Chevrolet, its descendants would have multiplied like rabbits.

Another look at Tom Griffith's flawless '64 Studebaker Avanti. Note the large-diameter dual exhausts riding low under the body extensions that covered the spring shackles of the modified Lark convertible chassis. Blade-type bumpers looked frail but proved surprisingly sturdy. License plate is at odds with actual 1964 production total.

we have sat in for many a day." It was a reasonable reaction from people who'd long doubted the sporting abilities of domestic iron, and the analysis was fair. In street form the Avanti was exactly what it was designed to be: a civilized, high-speed grand touring car, not a sports car.

Unfortunately, production woes thwarted the promise of the Avanti design. MFG had set its molds without due consideration for the expansion/contraction properties of curing fiberglass, and the first 100 or so bodies were hopelessly botched. Says engineer Otto Klausmeyer: "The doors wouldn't close, the hoods were out of line, the fender contours were mismatched. When we tried to drop the rear window into position it fell through the hole! We had to construct elaborate jigs to measure and compensate for the discrepancies and rush them to Ashtabula...Meanwhile, we bought a batch of power saws to cut up and refit all the early bodies."

The reason for this catastrophe has

less to do with MFG than with Sherwood Egbert, who by 1963 was employing desperation tactics to keep the company going. Remember that the car had been shown a year before, but thus far none had made it to dealers. He needed Avantis and he needed them in a hurry for the car to do its job as Studebaker's image-polisher, so he rushed production to maintain the public's high initial interest in it. The plan backfired badly, and was rendered hopeless when it turned out that buyer demand was not nearly as high as predicted. "Although we had very serious body difficulties, they were soon overcome," continues Klausmeyer—who was there. "We still had unsold Avantis all over the shop and in dealers' hands. This car was probably the poorest selling new job that Studebaker ever built." Only 3834 of the '63 models and 809 of the '64s were produced. (There is no dividing line other than registration date; see sidebar for the running changes made in the cars.)

Controversy has long raged over

whether the Avanti didn't sell because it took too long to reach customers or because customers didn't want it. The point is moot, because even Egbert knew that such a specialized car could never be built in really high volume. The Avanti's real purpose was to inspire—to make people believe that a faltering Studebaker wasn't faltering at all, that it was in business to stay. The planned follow-up, a whole new generation of Avanti-like sedans, was serious (the two mock-ups Loewy had built still exist in South Bend) but the public knew little of this. In retrospect, the Avanti's main handicap was that it was a Studebaker, the product of a company caught in an inexorable downward spiral of diminishing public confidence. Had it been a Chevrolet, its descendants would have multiplied like rabbits.

Sherwood Egbert left Studebaker in November 1963, ill with cancer, his hopes shattered. Before the year was out, his successors announced the end of production in South Bend. Manufacturing was then transferred entirely to a rump operation in Hamilton, Ontario, and both the Avanti and the GT Hawk were dropped. The last Studebakers, offered for 1965-66, were plain-jane sedans, coupes, and wagons powered by Chevy-built engines. With that, the Avanti was looking like an orphan child, the right stuff from the wrong company. But nobody counted on Nathan D. Altman.

Nate Altman, along with his partner Leo Newman, ran one of the country's most successful Studebaker dealerships—in downtown South Bend. For Nate, the demise of Studebaker was sad, but the loss of its most inspired creation was tragic. "I just couldn't let the Avanti die," he told this writer in 1971. "I started knocking on doors. You wouldn't *believe* the doors I knocked on." Altman first started knocking in Detroit, where he tried to convince the big automakers to pick up the rights and produce the Avanti. "None of them would touch it," he said ruefully. "Not even American Motors, who could have used it. I got desperate, so I paid a call on Morris Markin at Checker [the taxicab builder] in Kalamazoo. Know what he said? 'Mr. Altman, how can you expect Checker Motors to be interested in such an ugly car?' That was something, coming from the builder of the Checker Marathon! I walked out."

By 1964, Studebaker had put everything up for sale in South Bend. In February, Nate took matters into his own hands: he purchased two of the old buildings, with 500,000 square feet of floor space, and secured MFG's agreement to continue supplying Avanti body panels. Next, he asked Eugene Hardig to be his chief engineer. Hardig, nearing retirement, told Altman he had rocks in his head. Nate replied, "All your life you were told to cut corners to save 50 bucks to make a car cheaper. Here's your chance to build the best possible car without worrying about that." Hardig phoned him the next day to say, "Count me in." (Later, the taciturn Hardig could be made to admit that "I never had so

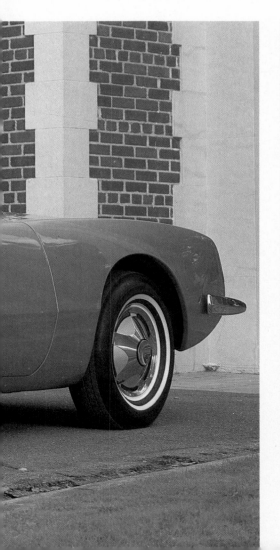

Running Changes to the Original Avanti, 1962-63

Jul 62: Improved rear window fastening

Sep 62: Revised rear shock absorbers

Oct 62: Baffled mufflers available

Mar 63: Light/heater switchplate redesigned. Rain drip molding added.

May 63: Optional interior offered with Tenite woodgrain panels, woodgrain steering wheel, all-black upholstery and "S-in-oblong" door panel ornaments.

Jun 63: Tenite panels and woodgrain wheel phased in as standard.

Aug 63: Rear quarter window latch redesigned. Stronger hinge for console box lid. Console control handles round instead of flat. Rubber door sill plate redesigned. Headlamp bezels changed from round to square. Parking lights restyled. Radiator grille added. Hood support moved from left to right. Air intake grille added to left side of cowl. Air duct to automatic transmissions on cars without a/c. Long battery replaced by standard-shaped battery. Valve-lifter cover (center valley plate) painted, not chromed. Inside air intake openings given plastic grilles. Solid-color interiors (including black) standard. Inside door panel "S" emblems standard. Rear window fastening again redesigned. Pleated "Regal" vinyl upholstery standard (previously optional). Perforated deluxe vinyl upholstery dropped. Carpet option reduced to black only. Fender plate changed to read "Supercharged Avanti" instead of "Supercharged."

Sep 63: Electric window cable shield added to cable between body and door. Manifold pressure gauge face redesigned. Thicker padding for bucket seat backs.

Dec 63: Factory announced phase-out of production (Production actually ceased in November).

Studebaker viewed the Avanti as subject to running changes rather than model year alterations. Contrary to common belief, for example, Avantis with square headlamp bezels do not constitute the entire run of 1964 models, since some registered '64s have round headlamp bezels. This list of significant Avanti changes by month was complied by Fred K. Fox.

Left: This was more or less the standard Avanti II interior treatment for 1982, though Altman would install any trim materials a customer desired. Opposite page, top: Here's the car that showed the author how much Avanti II quality had lapsed in the years since Nate Altman's death. Bottom: A more appealing early-Seventies example, here with Magnum 500 wheels.

much fun with anything as the Avanti II.")

Newman and Altman purchased the Avanti program, including all rights, equipment and parts, on July 1, 1964. The Avanti Motor Corporation was born, held by the two partners, the Altman family and several outsiders. Altman secured a line of credit, purely on his good name and the promise of a financially conservative operation. He announced that the car would henceforth be known as the "Avanti II," and through his first model year, 1965, he amazed onlookers as his factory turned out 45 of them.

Altman's greatest immediate problem was finding a new powerplant, because Studebaker in Hamilton had quit making the old 289 V-8. He and Hardig ended up choosing the ubiquitous Chevrolet 327 V-8 with 300 bhp, which was considerably lighter and yielded better handling. The rest of the car was built largely from existing Avanti parts. Altman did decide to make the front wheel openings smaller and to raise the front end, thus eliminating the noticeable forward rake of the original. "The people

I sell to aren't hot-rodders," he explained, and he hardly ever promoted the Avanti II as a high-performance car. Yet, in the beginning certainly, the 327 was more than enough: 0-60 mph came up in 7.5 seconds. Later, in 1969, the detoxed 350-cid engine was adopted and, still later, in the late 1970s, the Chevy 305—all in the interests of meeting government regulations. Straightline performance naturally suffered, but this never troubled Altman, who saw the car primarily as a limited-production luxury tourer.

To that end, Altman reformulated the Avanti as a virtually custom-built car. I can recall him now, on the phone in his corner office at South Bend, wheedling his sales prospects over the wires—which was the only way Nate sold cars. "Oh yes, doctor, we can upholster your car in Spanish suede. What color would you like? Your wife is deciding? Well, just have her send us a swatch and we'll do the rest...You say you want it painted chartreuse, doctor? Why of course we can do it. Shag carpets? No problem. D'you want 100-percent nylon or a blend?" He was a lovely man, one in a

million. To watch him at work was a unique experience.

There was no problem recruiting skilled workers at Avanti, for there were a great many rattling around South Bend in those early years following Studebaker's shutdown. The average age of Avanti workers then was 60 (it has since come down dramatically), and they weren't hurried. "If it takes them four hours to hang a door, right, it takes four hours," wrote one reporter at the time. "The workers are said to take it as a personal insult if fault is found with something they've done."

To match his custom-built approach Altman, together with veteran line man Harold Simmons, came up with a unique "bay system" production line. This is still largely followed by Avanti Motors' current management, although the setup has been rearranged for greater efficiency. At first it was strictly trial and error, Simmons said: "We didn't have any conveyors, we moved the cars by hand. On a big production line a man gets maybe two seconds to put a bolt in. If it doesn't get in, it doesn't. It takes us three to six weeks to do a car now, but Stude was building 20 Avantis a day."

Nate Altman liked nothing better than to tell visitors about his mini empire. "I don't believe there's any place in America where you'll find a completely integrated small manufacturing setup like Avanti Motor Corporation," he told this writer. "We have a complete miniaturized automobile factory. There isn't a bolt or washer or nut changed without the same degree of thoroughness you'd find in Detroit. We're making a lot of changes all the time but they're not being made haphazardly—they're tested, engineered. When you think of the size of our organization, I think you can appreciate how proud we all are of it, every one of us. We're producing a true craftsmanlike job. Therein lies, in this age of mass production, a unique story."

Above: The Avanti lives! Shown is the 1984 model with the specifications used for the first 50 production examples. Alterations made under the new Steve Blake regime include rectangular headlamps, body-color trim, a return to Loewy's original front-end rake and—a key spotter's point—bumper-mounted turn indicators. Opposite page: Spot the differences between the '84 and this 1983 20th Anniversary Edition model.

So it went, year in, year out, and each year Nate would squeeze out a few more Avanti IIs than he had the year before. Above all, he insisted on quality. Those early IIs were brilliant testimony to Altman, his workers, and their mutual dedication. They proved that a small company with limited resources could, after all, work noticeable improvements on something a much larger outfit had spent millions creating. In 1968 Avanti Motors had its first 100-car year, and by 1976 it had passed the 150-unit level. Unfortunately, that proved to

be the high-water mark for the Altman concern, for that was the year Nate died. His successors were much less careful.

Government regulations streamed out of Washington like ants at a picnic in the 1970s, and small automakers like Avanti were especially hard-hit. Contrary to what many of us believed, specialty cars were by no means exempt from the majority of emissions, fuel economy and safety standards. Lacking Nate Altman's innate sense of quality and his efficient solutions to problems, Avanti Motors turned to meeting these requirements with patchwork engineering—like sticking on ugly modified bumpers to comply with barrier crash standards. Although performance was never the II's main selling point, it naturally fell as emission controls began to choke down the big V-8s. More importantly, quality began to fall at the same time even as prices rose dramatically. The

Avanti II that had sold for $6550 in "base" form back in 1965 was well up into five figures by the time Nate Altman died. By the 1980s it was over $20,000, a level where the Avanti faced formidable competition from better organized, more experienced and, in some cases, larger specialty manufacturers like Jaguar, BMW, and Porsche.

Just how far the Avanti II had fallen was born out by a 1982 model tested by the editors in early 1983. The paint had more ripples in it than a village bondo job; a poorly prepared surface showed through thinly plated bumpers; there were several things falling off or coming unglued inside; the shag carpets, so popular in Nate Altman's day, now looked horribly passé. The handling reminded us of a brontosaurus with dyspepsia. The car wasn't very fast, but it had a heavy thirst. There wasn't a member of our staff who would give a dime for that

Once again, the Avanti is exquisitely put together with the best-quality materials money can buy and, consequently, feels about as substantial as the Washington Monument. The basic body design remains good-looking even after 20 years.

'82—nor bet on the long-term survival of Avanti Motors.

But help was just around the corner. It came in the person of a dynamic young building contractor and car nut from Washington D.C., Stephen H. Blake. He not only purchased Avanti Motors but instituted a wholesale housecleaning as vigorous in its way as Sherwood Egbert's mop-up at Studebaker back in 1961.

Blake grew up in Baltimore, where his father sold Buicks—and laughingly warned him, "Kid, don't *ever* follow in my footsteps." After a stint in the Marine Corps in the mid-Sixties, and a distasteful bout as a Humble Oil management trainee, Blake joined a booming construction firm and worked his way up from ditchdigger to regional manager. He learned enough to launch his own real estate development company in 1969, and over the next eight years put together 25 deals totaling $147 million. "Real estate," he said, "taught me how to pull order out of chaos."

After all but camping on Avanti's doorstep for six or seven years, Blake purchased the company from the Altman family in October 1982. From there, as the accompanying interview reveals, it's been a steady if often exhausting process of renewal and improvement for South Bend's now 21-year-old *gran turismo*.

DRIVING IMPRESSIONS

How good is it, really? To summarize the 1984 Avanti (Blake has dropped the Roman numeral "II") in one sentence, it's a car that shows its age through certain design shortcomings, but is, again, exquisitely put together with the best-quality materials money can buy and, consequently, feels about as substantial as the Washington Monument.

It's obvious almost at once that the engineering hasn't changed much in 20 years. The windshield sits at an angle that's unfashionably upright now. The new white-on-black Stewart-Warner instruments look better than the dials previously used, but their chrome bezels almost scream "1963." There's no face-level ventilation; pull on one of the chrome vent toggles and you get a blast of cold air that freezes your feet. The car sits rather high off the road, although it doesn't *look* high, and despite all the glass, visibility isn't great by current standards. All these things and others are, of course, expected in a car conceived almost a quarter-century ago. It is a tribute to Loewy, Andrews, Kellogg and Ebstein that the basic Avanti body design remains so good-looking and right-feeling all these many years later.

And it does, you know—it really does. That shape was well nigh unimprovable for its time, and Blake has

Today's Avanti looks as purposeful and powerful as the original. High-performance low-profile tires are new, but wheel openings remain the same size as on the Avanti II.

wisely decided not to make any major changes in the styling. He has restored the original front-end rake, partly because market surveys reveal that Avanti's customers are not, at least not anymore, the greybeard types Nate Altman fancied them to be. Their average age is 42—less than Porsche's, less than Jaguar's. The rake looks good. And it's *supposed* to be there.

The improvements Blake has engineered into the car are tremendously impressive, even more so considering he's been calling the shots for such a short time. Finish is spectacular, about as good as that of any fiberglass-body car found anywhere, including the latest Corvette. The new body-color bumpers are very *au courant*, but get mixed reviews. They look better to us on the red and silver cars than they do on the more extreme white and black jobs. In any case, if you insist, you can still order a set of chrome-plated ones, though you'll have to put 'em on yourself.

On the inside, Blake's team has worked a minor revolution. No more shag carpets, no more dinky dials and afterthought switchgear, no more woodgrain. Everything is now very businesslike: the instruments, honest and straightforward, are set into a flat-black panel, and minor controls are positioned for easy access and work logically. A few familiar Avanti features like the glovebox vanity and the rear parcel shelf trap door have been eliminated. But a lot of really snazzy items have been added: smashing Recaro bucket seats with so many adjustments you can virtually custom-set your favorite position, a purposeful leather-wrapped steering wheel (a wood-rim Nardi wheel is optional), a first-rate electric moonroof. Our only significant cockpit criticism involves the aforementioned lack of modern face-level ventilation. Whether this can be incorporated in the future without changing the basic panel is questionable, but we hope it can. We're also not sure about the decision to replace the vinyl dashboard top covering with leather. The hide looks and feels nice but doesn't lend itself to the complex curves of the Avanti dash, and on the '84s we ob-

served it seems rather lumpy. Also, leather is more prone to cracking and fading than vinyl, and demands more frequent care, too.

It isn't really fair to record performance figures. The present 175-bhp engine will be phased out in favor of a 200-bhp 305 V-8 early in 1984 and final drive gearing will be a bit shorter, both of which will help off-the-line snap. The current car is geared high and is not particularly quick from a standing start. Our stopwatch tests gave 11 seconds for 0-60 mph, which still isn't bad. High-speed cruising, on the other hand, is ultra-smooth and quiet—and mileage is fantastic. The Avanti's EPA city/highway fuel economy numbers are better than for any other low-production specialty car; in fact, it's the only one that avoids the federal gas guzzler tax, and by quite a wide margin. Most drivers should average 23-24 mpg overall. The distance between fuel stops is probably more important to the Avanti buyer than mpg figures, but it's nice to know that all this luxury does not come with the penalty of excessive thirst, even with a V-8.

Few Avanti owners will ask more of their car's handling than the '84 can deliver. There must have been a lot of work done here, because the latest model feels totally different from the '82 we drove a year ago: flat, stable, with predictable and safe understeer. The brakes pull up the car with authority even after several successive applications from 70 mph.

All these improvements aren't free, of course. We've been told, but have not yet confirmed, that some dealers are getting well above sticker due to the current, very high demand. Even so, the 1984 car at $36,000 is a lot better value, in our view, than the '82 was at under $30,000. This isn't, after all, a lot to pay for a hand-built car, let alone one backed by so much obvious dedication.

For the first time in years, the Avanti has a future. And it looks to be a rosy one indeed.

Avanti Model Year Production 1965 to Date							
1965	45	1970	117	1975	125	1980	168
1966	59	1971	107	1976	156	1981	195
1967	66	1972	127	1977	146	1982	188
1968	100	1973	106	1978	165	1983	276
1969	92	1974	123	1979	142	1984	360-400 (est.)

What's Steve Blake Really Like?

An Interview with
Stephen H. Blake
by Richard Langworth, Graham
Robson, and the Editors of
Collectible Automobile™.

Entering the sanctum of the president, chief executive officer and board chairman of the sixth largest car company in America, you know immediately that things are a little different at Avanti Motors than they are at General Motors.

Stephen H. Blake sits behind an old steel desk piled high with papers, telephone books, ashtrays and odd car parts. The walls are covered by the sort of paneling you buy at Sears for your hunting lodge in the Poconos. Enormous, ancient pipework ducts a trickle of hot water to a solitary radiator, but the holes around the old window air conditioner overwhelm this modest source of heat and you shiver. "I had a space heater in here but I gave it to the secretaries," Blake apologizes over a cup of coffee the consistency of treacle. "You gotta take care of the help first."

Blake rarely wears a tie around the plant, let alone the three-piece Brooks Brothers suit that is de rigueur in the more splendid offices up in Detroit. He usually sports a navy blue pullover and a pair of faded khaki trousers. He chain smokes, interrupting his running dialogue on the second rebirth of Avanti with telephone calls and fitful stabs at his mail. "What the hell is this b.s.?" he says to himself as he opens another letter. "Look at this junk!" He holds up a piece of corrugated black plastic with a silver

mylar trim strip. "We asked these clowns to send us some samples of a better trim strip, and they send us this garbage! I'm gonna have to give those birds a piece of my mind."

The chairman of Avanti Motor Corporation has begun another perfect day at South Bend, heart of the universe, his windswept corner office part of an ancient building that was once part of a mammoth automobile complex. Outside, cold blasts with that special chill found only in the Midwest gust around the derelict empire of crumbling brick that still marks the remains of Studebaker, unlikely creator of the Avanti, the car that will not die.

The following is the result of two interviews conducted with Steve Blake, which give as complete a picture of the Avanti as you'll find anywhere in print. Blake is, perforce, controversial. There are those who call him a visionary, the saviour of his company, a car nut, a fantastic salesman and the prince of optimists. And then there are those who call him a lot of other things. About Steve Blake there is no shortage of opinions, no lack of descriptions. But there is no one who says he is not interesting.

Personally, we like him immensely. There's no blather in his conversation, no dodging questions, no monkey motion or platitudes. Blake admits to problems with a candor unknown in the guarded citadels of Detroit. He's enthusiastic about his car and sanguine about its future, but he won't tell you any part of it is the greatest unless he is absolutely convinced it is so.

This is Steve Blake's story in his own words, punctuated with as many pointed questions as we were able to hurl at him. We can't help but think that, after reading this, you'll probably wish him as much luck for the future as we do.

All the best, Steve. —RML

CA: What's a smart guy like you doing here in South Bend?
Blake: Gee, I don't know why I can't get more people to move here, from places like Monterey and Miami...

I got involved kind of by default. I'd been a car lover, fancier, buff, nut, whatever you call it, for many years. I think the first car I ever bought was a '49 Studebaker two-door business coupe. When I got out of college the first car I bought was a '57 T-Bird. It was in 1966. I'd wanted something really neat and I paid like $6-7000 for it. Then I started collecting T-Birds; I've probably owned about 10. Later I started playing around with Italian cars, and they were another story altogether. They're really nice to look at and drive once in awhile, but you don't drive them *all* the time. Around late '72 I was driving a Maserati Ghibli—or I should say *trying* to drive one. One morning it just wouldn't go. And, dammit, I had a whole bunch of other cars in the garage and none of *them* would go, either. So I took a cab to work.

I was in the building business, and I had to have a car I could drive every day. I called some friends and asked for advice; I wanted something really good-looking but reliable. You think about reliability and you're going to buy an American car, of course. Somebody said, "Well, you know they're still building the Avanti," and I said "What? I didn't know that!" To make a long story short, I found a used one and drove it for a couple of years, every day. I kept my Italian junk, and probably added more junk by then. But I just couldn't believe the Avanti. It was super. It really broke less than any car I'd ever owned. It even started every morning, which was novel. The streets in Washington, D.C., where I was working, weren't always the greatest, but the car held up very well. And this was an *old* Avanti II, a '68 or '69 with, I think, 90,000 miles—a D.C. car that had been driven hard.

In late 1974 or early '75 I bought a new one. I came out here and couldn't believe they were building cars here. It just floored me. How did they get them out? How did it get done? It just didn't make any sense. It took me years to learn just how they managed to get them out the door at this place. Naturally I ordered the car over the phone from Nate Altman. The reason I had to come pick it up was because he wouldn't deliver it. He said, "You've been an Avanti owner for three years and you've never seen the plant. If you want the damn car you've got to come out here." I told him, "You've got my money, now I want the car." Nate said "No." I fell madly in love with Nate Altman. He was a beauty, know what I mean? He was a classic, one of the great characters of all time. So we kept in touch.

Around February '76 I sent the car back

47

> "Finally, Arnold Altman said, 'Look, do me a favor: stop calling me. Either come out here and buy the company or leave me alone.' I was here the next morning."

out to have an automatic installed. I had the last four-speed they ever built and my left leg was getting too muscular because Nate used about an 11½-inch truck clutch. In fact my right leg is still smaller than my left leg. The same thing happened: he wouldn't send it back! He wanted me to come out and get it. But this time he said he wanted to talk to me.

I came out and he asked if I wanted to buy the company. He was in his late 60s; he had no one to turn the business over to. His son is a doctor, his daughter was married to another builder like me, his partner had a parts business. He said, "I've got to do something, because one of these days I'm going to die." We were seriously discussing things, and had made plans to get together after he returned from a vacation in Europe. He went to Europe and dropped dead.

CA: Why didn't you get the company then and there?

Below: They still build cars the old-fashioned way at Avanti, though the aging plant is being reorganized for greater efficiency as one of the Blake regime's many reforms.

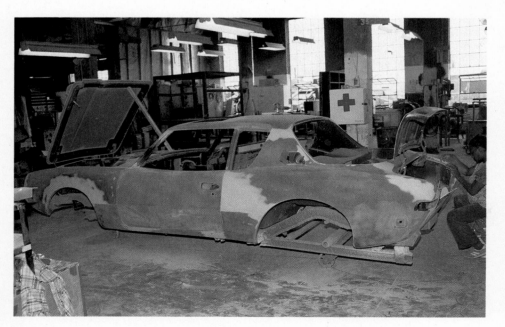

Blake: Because it was like talking to a wall. Nate's family didn't know what to do. There were 14 shareholders, 11 of them family members. Nobody agreed, there were lawsuits and countersuits. Nate's brother Arnold was in charge, but he wouldn't talk to me. I'm very tenacious, and I kept after him. I really loved the car, you have to understand that. I felt this was the only company of its nature, and that it had a future. It needed updating and improvement, that's all.

CA: You had to be tenacious to keep after them for four years...
Blake: Right. And by 1980 it was really looking sad for the car. Things had been added to meet the government regulations, but the quality of the workmanship, the body, the interior were going downhill. Meanwhile, I'd gotten involved in the automobile business in Newport, New Hampshire, and I'd observed that the specialty cars like Corvette, Ferrari, Jaguar kept selling even when the general car business was bad. So I knew the Avanti could survive.

CA: Weren't there other people who tried to buy the company?
Blake: Sure, there were a lot of them, but they couldn't stand dealing with these people. It was that simple. But I was determined. I kept calling Arnold. Finally he said, "Look, do me a favor, stop calling me. Either come out here and buy the business or leave me alone." I was here the next morning.

CA: Was it like you remembered it from your earlier visits?
Blake: Worse! First of all you never saw anybody working.

CA: Does that mean you have fewer people on the payroll now?

Blake: No. It's within four or five of the same number, because we added a second shift to the machine and paint shops, and I put a management team together. The difference is that they're all working hard now.

CA: Were they ready to sell out, then?
Blake: Yes and no. I had the problem of dealing with 14 people, which was incredible. It took us until July 1982 to come up with a price—from about October 1980. It took us four months to get the letter of intent signed. We started negotiating the contract in September, and then I had to start looking for financing.

CA: The figure was $4,050,000 in one article. Is that right?
Blake: Not exactly, but it's close enough. But you know what it was like looking for financing for an auto manufacturing business in 1981? They looked at you like you had leprosy. Meanwhile, it got to be February '82 and we still hadn't signed the contract. My lawyers were getting sick and I was paying my lawyers. I can't think of how many times I should have walked away. I really had to *want* this business.

In May or June '82, I heard that Indiana was putting together a guarantee program, long-term. I talked to them, and then I went to a bank here, and we were able to put a loan together. We finally signed the agreement around the end of July, and we took over here on October 1st, 1982.

CA: Was the company making money?
Blake: Just about. It's just peanuts. They made a little bit every year, they were always in the black.

CA: Are we talking a million?
Blake: Naw!

CA: $500,000?
Blake: Naw!

CA: $100,000?
Blake: Barely. Every year it was like that. They sold a few more parts, a few more cars. A lot of the sales, 60 percent, were to repeat customers.

CA: What did you do first?
Blake: I don't remember. There was so much to do all at once! But by December 31st I'd cleaned house. Doesn't matter. The skeletons are *still* coming out of the closet. I'm sure we'll get one today. They come absolutely every day!

Anyway, we asked all the management to leave. It was a carnival. I'd be here to 11, 12 at night trying to bring some order. By the end of the first month the only guy I'd brought with me was giving his notice. He was an industry executive type, used to GM, and he couldn't take it. He stayed for about five months.

At the end of the first month I figured I had lost my mind. My emotions had carried me along in buying the business, but I had to be nuts. I needed help. I have a friend who is a lawyer. He was in Newport, N.H. but he'd moved to California. He was unquestionably the best detail man I'd ever met, period—*and* he was a car nut. I called him on his boat at Marina del Rey and said, "John, how would you like to come to South Bend?" He said, "Are you out of your mind?" I said, "But John, we're building cars—it's really neat!" He said, "Blake, I've known you too long. Do you need me?" I said, "Yup." He said, "I'll be there in three days." He's *still* here.

CA: What about the workforce?
Blake: I shocked the living hell out of them. I told them, "You're supposed to come to work at 7 o'clock. If you're not here, you're fired." Lee Iacocca was my hero. I also went out there on the floor and worked with the people every day. I told them, "It's real simple. Your wages stink. I don't know if you know that or not." They knew it. I said, "But you don't *work* for them. You're not even worth what you get paid. *I* wouldn't work for these kind of wages, and I'm the boss. But if you'd like to make some money, you're going to have to get to work and get this place organized."

CA: That's probably where you crossed the union. Avanti has never been unionized and we understand you've kept it that way.
Blake: We beat them this time. You see, I fired a bunch of people, so there were a lot of them who didn't like me. Indiana is a very pro-union state—very. The majority of businesses in this town are unionized. UAW is not very fond of me right now. We put in work rules. They are very simple. You come to work. You do your job. If you can't do it, come tell us. We'll help you, we'll train you. If you don't like your job, we'll find you another one here. Just try. Don't lie to us. . . And come to work.

CA: Did they buy it?
Blake: Well, the first four months were pretty interesting. I kept saying to myself, "How did this business get by? I mean, how did they get these cars out?" I finally found out when we were getting the racing car ready for Daytona. A week and a half before the race we were so far from being ready it was pathetic. We got all our mechanics and body people together and told them what the problem was, and they pulled three all-nighters in a row. They caught a couple of hours sleep in shifts. They slept in the cars, on the floor. They pulled together and got it done. We were loading the car on the trailer at 7 o'clock on a Saturday morning and it hit me: *that's how the cars got built!* The workers would go ask for directions and they 'wouldn't get an answer. So they said screw it, and they went and did it themselves. They didn't have any choice. When Nate was here, of

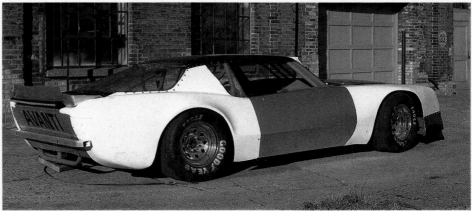

course, they got an answer.

I took that into consideration. The dignity of the worker is very important to me. I learned that in the construction business, from a real tyrant. He'd give you impossible things to do and you'd say, "That crazy s.o.b." But he always treated you with respect. The workforce responded. And we went out and found supervisors, professionals. We stole a guy from Bendix, we stole a guy from AM General—good people.

CA: This racing program. . .
Blake: What racing program?

CA: Well, you ran at Daytona in 1983. Are you going to keep going with that, or was it just for fun?
Blake: If we can get somebody to pay for it. No, it wasn't for fun, it was for business. But we had some people pay for some of it. The Daytona car was built by a good friend of mine who works for us now, Herb Adams, who had a hand in the Pontiac Trans Am. We hired a short-track chassis builder to build us a chassis. We had a lot of breaks. The engine builder donated all his labor, and we got the engine done for about $9000 with all kinds of stuff from Chevrolet. Goodyear gave us tires, the transmission people gave us transmissions, Dayton gave us wheels. We finished, which was respectable. I sure didn't want to make a fool of myself, and with their help I didn't. We would like to

Above: A surprise entry at Daytona in 1983 was this Avanti racer prepared by chassis wizard Herb Adams. Future track outings are uncertain, but some of Adams's work is being applied to an all-new 1985 chassis.

do it again, but it's really expensive for us. We need some biggies to sponsor us. I can't tell you what's going to happen in the near future.

CA: We think it's a gangbuster NASCAR stocker.
Blake: It's the right size, too. But they've got certain minimum requirements in terms of volume. The only one we need is IMSA. We've won one IMSA race, so who knows?

The racing story was really a reflection of the big picture itself. We wanted certain types of guys. One of my requirements was that they had to be car nuts. We found our manufacturing guy in Florida, we found our comptroller in Michigan, we found one of our engineers in Pittsburgh. And I offered them life in this wonderful place. . .How could they go wrong, with low pay, long hours and hard work?

CA: You've said your policy was based on "people, product, and distribution." You've talked about people. What about the product?
Blake: Where do I begin?

CA: On the outside and work in.
Blake: We changed our paint system in

"I would almost prefer the Avanti to be the American Rolls-Royce with Porsche characteristics. I'm not trying to copy anyone."

January. They were getting lousy body panels from the stamper, Molded Fiberglass in Ashtabula, Ohio. They'd always been lousy. But I found out more. Way back, 10 years ago, somebody recommended that they start using this type of filler instead of getting good body panels. Just smear this crap all over the body and sand it off, okay? Right. Just hours and hours of work. Somebody said they weren't putting enough on, so they put *more* on. Customers would have a little accident and their lawyers would want to sue because you sold them a used car that had been wrecked: the whole body was filled with filler! *The whole schmear!* Know what? We took a body and didn't put *any* filler in it. Just went ahead and painted it. *It didn't look bad!* So for years and years they'd been spending 80 to 100 hours putting this crap all over the bodies for no reason.

CA: You're not going to say all the obvious improvement in body finish quality was due to removing the filler...
Blake: No, it has to do with paint, too. The old plant manager had the idea that he should use enamel primer. Well, you don't put lacquer on enamel, although you can put enamel on lacquer. I said this was all wrong. Now we're using a new paint from Ditzler called Deltron, which is the highest tech paint there is. It looks like

lacquer, but it wears like iron. I started doing some reading and making some calls, and I found it. It is *unreal.*

CA: You're the first to use it. How new is it?
Blake: This year.

CA: Just this year?
Blake: There have been polyurethane paints, like Imron, around for seven, eight years. This Deltron is far more advanced. It doesn't require the constant care that lacquer does. For example, you can't get gasoline on lacquer or it'll eat through it. The Ditzler people poured gasoline all over this Deltron and let it sit overnight. Nothing. The stuff is unbelievable.

CA: You also leaned on Ashtabula for better body panels, right?
Blake: Absolutely. The body technology is some 30 years old, and they like the old technology at Ashtabula. But there's been three stages of improvement over the years. Right now, the Pontiac Fiero is state-of-the-art in terms of body materials. We thought and thought, and two months ago our new body panels were delivered, which are essentially the same material as the '84 Corvette's.

CA: What about the recent cars with the old, low-tech paint jobs?
Blake: We had a terrific problem—90 percent of our warranty claims. The only cars still using lacquer are Rolls and Ferrari. People don't drive those every day, but the Avanti is an everyday car. The first two weeks I was here I had them wet-sanding every car. Twenty cars sitting out back weren't sold; I wouldn't let them out. We went back and reshot and wet buffed every one.

CA: Now tell us about the interior.
Blake: We knew what the easy problems were: carpeting and upholstery. We went to probably as good a leather as you can buy anywhere. We got rid of those shag carpets they used to use and installed nice, plush Antron with a 10-year wear guarantee. We changed wheels: we went back to Nardi for our optional wheel and used a leather-wrapped wheel as standard. We got a lot of Mickey Mouse stuff out of the car. We cleaned up the switch panel above the header, and the power door locks are in the doors where they belong. Those damn toggle switches are all gone from under the dash. You'd put your finger under there and there were all kinds of switches. I don't know what the hell they were for. In the upper switch panel we'll soon have four single switches: lights, heater, moonroof, rear window defroster. We got rid of that thing you cut your fingers on to unlock the door and put a regular little safety pull in the corner. Don't ask me where those things came from.

CA: They were very stylish in 1963...
Blake: They weren't even *there* in 1963. We've cleaned up the dash, too. Our shifter ball's bigger, more comfortable. The dash is now leather. We have a new Blaupunkt radio. We're the first in the world to use it, with a zowie speaker and radio system.

CA: The new Recaro seats are a major improvement on the old, shallow buckets.
Blake: That's the electric one with all the buttons. Recaro is now building seats in Ligonier, Indiana, 60 miles from here, which is a big plus for us. But we're going through the big changeover and there're all kinds of problems, so for the first 50 cars they made a deal with us to give us that $1500 seat. I mean we're going to have $3000 worth of seats in the car.

CA: What about color schemes?
Blake: The first 50 '84s will be Avanti's colors: silver, red, white, and blue. These all have the new body-color bumpers, which are indestructible urethane-based plastic.

CA: But will you also continue the policy of allowing the customer to select colors?
Blake: Oh yes. That's easy and fun, no problem. But realistically speaking, 99 percent of the cars get built with about 10 different interiors and 15 exterior colors.

CA: So you're not getting that many wild color orders?
Blake: Not any more. The wildest we had was for a guy on the Board of Regents at the University of Michigan—blue and yellow.

CA: We saw it in back. It's certainly cheerful.
Blake: We had another for Palm Beach in bright green leather and paint. Funny—it wasn't that bad! The thought is nauseating, but when the car was all done it looked good. Bright, but good.

CA: Why did you switch from the traditional bumper design to the body-color type?
Blake: It began with quality. The chrome looked bad—rippled, poorly finished. I sent a spec to a high-dollar show chrome plater. He called back amazed, saying the spec was 20, 30 years old. We couldn't afford the old process to do it right. I asked him what he would recommend and he said, "chrome is for Duesenbergs. Go to a polished aluminum or stainless." It finally materialized that a set of bumpers done right could cost $400, which wasn't so bad when you realize that a big Olds bumper costs $800 today. But this was still using the old specs.

The '82 bumpers weren't original anyway. They had this thing with two rubber pods on it to meet the 5-mph crash spec. It didn't meet the 2½-mph corner spec, but they had an exemption. When the govern-

Converted from a 1977 coupe, this is the prototype for the '84 convertible, which will be phased in with the latest production modifications.

ment dropped the spec from 5 to 2½ front/rear and 2½ to 1.75 mph on the corners, believe it or not that horrible old bumper met it!

Even so, we decided by then to redesign the bumper. We came up with a high-tech plastic, but this failed even the new 2½-mph spec. Dammit, I was *not* going to put that chrome bumper back on. We decided to go with a box-section Kevlar, made by DuPont—energy absorbing—which met the 5-mph test. The corners make 2 mph, which is more than we need. I'm not crazy about it, but something had to be done. And it's strong. You can't break or twist it. While the basic design of future bumpers might stay similar, we are working on new systems.

CA: The traditionalists don't like the body-color bumpers.
Blake: The traditionalists don't buy our cars. They buy our parts, but not our cars. But if you were ordering a new Avanti and had to have the old bumpers, we'd sell them to you. You'd have to put them on yourself, though...

CA: Tell us about drivetrains. Start with the engine.
Blake: Coming in "1984½"—as soon as they start phasing in—is a new Chevrolet High-Output 305, about 200 horsepower. It gets incredible gas mileage, EPA 29

highway and 18 city. There isn't another V-8 that gets that. Excalibur, Rolls, Aston Martin are all paying the gas guzzler tax, but not Avanti. And it's more powerful than the present engine.

CA: How? Through carburetion?
Blake: That and some internal workings. We're making a change in the exhausts, the computer and some internal workings—cam, crank. Right now we have the LG4, which is about 175 bhp, and a real low rear end, so it's not fast off the line. You're going to do 0-60 mph times in under nine seconds, let's say. The new engine will improve on that.

CA: How much of the engine modification was Avanti's and how much was GM's?
Blake: They designed the engine; we manufactured the exhaust system and put our combination together with the transmission and rear end. The new 305 will be better than the carbureted 350. And I just don't want fuel injection.

CA: Too complex or costly?
Blake: Yes, and you're not going to get the same fuel economy, regardless of what people say. Not that fuel economy is a big item for the people buying our cars, but if the technology is there, why be a schmuck? That's what we did.

CA: And what else are you up to? We notice there's a "turbo" nameplate on your desk...
Blake: You didn't see that! You never know. Deciding what to improve...I don't know whether that'll occur or not.

See, performance is not just power. It's handling, braking...

CA: Well, what about the rest of the drivetrain, then?
Blake: I'm pleased. We had '56 Girling Jaguar brakes on the car, a little pad 1-inch square. We now have 11-inch GM ventilated discs on the front that knock 35 feet off our 70-0 mph panic stop. We had a lousy steering gear ratio—24:1, five-and-a-half turns lock-to-lock. We've improved that, and by late '84 we'll have a power rack. The Saginaw box we use is the best anywhere. So is the GM four-speed overdrive automatic—very smooth, the best anywhere. Jaguar and Aston Martin both use it.

CA: What about the new chassis that we understand is being engineered by Herb Adams?
Blake: We're prototyping now. We didn't have tooling for a lot of suspension parts, and it would take as much time to re-do the existing frame rails and cross-member as it would to start with a clean sheet of paper. So that's what we did. We're looking at a double-wishbone four-wheel independent suspension, with coil springs all around. We're in the development process, but it looks good.

CA: We assume weight-saving played a role in this redesign?
Blake: A lot—200, 300 pounds. The new chassis is light and much stronger. It has a backbone with frame rails and will carry the body three inches lower. We've got a power rack-and-pinion unit in front, four-

wheel discs, a lot of interesting stuff.

CA: You'll have to modify your floorpan, obviously.
Blake: We've already built the new one.

CA: Adding footwells? There's no legroom in back now.
Blake: Oh yes, we're adding 2½-3 inches to the floor. The backbone will provide an armrest. Basically you'll have four bucket seats. It may look different from what it looks like right now. We're track testing now. It may take an extra year, but the car is not going to be compromised.

CA: An important angle to collectors is the parts situation. Can they count on you?
Blake: Yes. But I have made some Avanti owners unhappy, because in June I put in an across-the-boards 50-percent increase in parts prices. The problem was that they'd forgotten to raise the price of the parts the last three years. Forgot! I had my parts manager come in with a pile of stuff and lay it on the table, and he had a sheet to say what this and that part cost us. We were selling parts for $70 that cost $150 to build. Chrome bumpers that cost us $200 apiece selling for $150. On this basis the parts operation wasn't very profitable at all. We didn't have any choice.

CA: People, product—now what about distribution?
Blake: They had a dealer network when I arrived: three dealers and about 40 people who'd sell a car now and then if they felt like it. If you came here to buy a car they'd make you a dealer. We sent all these "dealers" cancellation notices. It was ridiculous. They'd order cars and if they didn't feel like picking them up they wouldn't bother. The company received no deposits, there was no order system

We set up a network of 30 quality dealers this year, and we now have a real simple system. Each dealer gets us an open letter of credit for two cars at all times; or we have a line of credit agreement with their floorplan source; or they send us a deposit with each order. The cars don't leave here without being paid for. Right now we have a serious three-month backlog. Everything we're building is sold.

CA: Where are your major markets?
Blake: New York, south Florida, Chicago, Texas and California. We have completed recruiting in these places, except California.

CA: What's the average age of an Avanti buyer?
Blake: It's interesting. It's 42. What do you think the average age is of a Porsche buyer? It's 44. Jaguar's about 50. Cadillac Eldorado, 52. So the Avanti owner is, comparatively, young.

CA: And is this buyer a doctor or a lawyer, mainly?

Above: A first for Avanti is Deltron, a new long-wearing polyurethane paint. Here, a near-finished car bakes in the paint booth. Opposite page: Another look at one of the first 50 production '84s. Interior revisions mandated by Blake include standard Recaro Model C seats, leather dash top cover, relocated switchgear borrowed from GM, and low-pile nylon carpeting. Padded-rim leather-wrapped steering wheel is optional.

Blake: Nope. Most of them are repeat buyers, as I said. But a good 70 percent are entrepreneurs, people in business for themselves, involved in the arts, writing, directing, interior design, construction. Creative people. Lots of builders, developers. A lot of people think the Avanti is a cult car. It becomes a cult car after you buy it, not before. You buy it for other reasons: because you like its looks, because it's unique, because it feels solid, because it's built by hand.

CA: And the old Studebaker buffs? Do they buy cars?
Blake: As I said, no. Most people think they do, but they don't. First of all they can't afford it. There are some who can, of course, but they don't, as a rule, buy the cars. We're supporting the Studebaker clubs, but they don't buy our car. The demographics are very close to those of Jaguar, and frankly I was amazed, particularly at the percentage of repeat own-

ers: over 50-55 percent. I'm convinced that we've got a very loyal and strong owner body, and it's *these* people we have to take care of.

CA: Let's say everything works out. The skeletons come out of all the closets and you do everything you want to do and you have one helluva car. How many can you realistically build?
Blake: Guess.

CA: 500?
Blake: Higher!

CA: 600?
Blake: Higher!

CA: Surely not 1000?
Blake: Would you believe 1200?

CA: Without compromising anything?
Blake: Nothing. I'm not smart enough to figure these things out, so we hired the automotive manufacturing consulting division of Arthur Anderson & Co. They're

CA: Spilling back over into product, what can we expect in the immediate future? Will there be a four- or five-speed option?
Blake: Market research says that a very small number of high-priced sports cars are sold with five-speeds. Corvette's experience is 92 percent automatic. But we'll have one in the near future, as long as my ass is on the line. You have to understand: I'm a car nut and I want one. And there are car nuts who want it and won't buy a car without it. It's not that complicated. You have to run a separate EPA test. That's the hard part, and that's already been done.

CA: Of course, your new convertible is a big step forward.
Blake: The first model was built for the show circuit by Richard Straman of California. That's just the show car. Hopefully, by early 1984 we'll be building them.

CA: One of your managers told us the convertible would sell for between $40,000 and $60,000. That was as narrow as he wanted to guesstimate for now. But you obviously hope to make some money out of all this hard work, too.
Blake: It's not for exercise.

CA: One thing we have to ask. What does Raymond Loewy think?
Blake: He calls about once a month.

CA: What do you talk about?
Blake: He wants to redesign the car!

CA: How?
Blake: I don't know. I told him I can't afford it. But I have no interest in changing the basic design. It's like what Porsche did over the years with the 911. I mean, the 911's been out since 1964. They've changed trim, bumpers; they put some flares on, they changed the drivetrain. But the body's the same. And I think they did one hell of a job.

CA: Do you see the Avanti becoming something like an American Porsche, if not in design then in quality?
Blake: Well, what I think I'd like is to have a combination of things, and we can do that by model. I would almost prefer it to be the American Rolls-Royce with Porsche characteristics. I'm not trying to copy anyone.

CA: You're invoking Rolls-Royce here for craftsmanship, for luxury, or both?
Blake: Craftsmanship, luxury and quality. The way that Rolls used to be. Not the way they are now, which is sad. I've owned a Rolls, and it was lovely. I drove a new Spirit recently and it *wasn't* lovely. The only nice thing about it was the rack-and-pinion steering. I'm not fond of the new style. I think the old Cloud was much better, much better put together.

What I think we've got here is an opportunity to build the best car in America, possibly the world. It's not easy. But it can be done.

the best in this country—the people who went to Japan after the war and set up that industry. Their project leader, who's in his 60s, came here, studied our fixtures, and came up with a new layout which is about 65 percent done. They really got a kick out of this place, so they decided to make a project out of it. They're fabulous guys and they're *so smart.* I love working with smart people. They came up with two alternative layouts and said we can do 90 to 100 cars a month, somewhere around four cars a day. And of course we could sell them, since there was virtually no selling at all under the previous management.

CA: Is that your goal then? Twelve hundred a year?
Blake: To be safe, for '84 it's between 360 and 400. We want to do it slowly. But already our production and sales have increased by over 50 percent.

CA: In this past 10 months?
Blake: Yes. When I bought the company I had to budget for a lot of capital expenditures and not operating expenses. But the plan was there to do it and it's just being done. The place looks like a mess. You used to be able to walk in and see the body line and the chassis line, and it looked nice. The problem was that the car went from over there to over here to over here and back again. We had a running joke that the car was out of warranty before it left the factory! Looking at the ultimate plan, everything just flows nicely. We're in the process of moving all the chassis stuff now. Then the body line will be finished, and the new paint shop. We're working on all this nights and weekends, and we've put together a real maintenance and construction crew. Yet we haven't lost one bit of production. We're building 30 cars a month now, some months 35. So it's working, it's working.

The Collectible Avanti: A Shopper's Guide

In discussing the Avanti's merits as a collectible automobile it is important to distinguish between the Studebaker-built 1963-64 models and the subsequent 1965-82 cars built under the Nate Altman regime. All make satisfying collectibles, though for very different reasons. All are sought-after today; all have potential as high-return investments. But although they may look somewhat alike, these are two distinct model groups with decidedly individual characters. And while the car's basic engineering may not have changed much in 25 years, the numerous alterations made in mechanical components, construction methods, equipment and materials over the years have a real bearing on asking prices, value appreciation, desirability, even condition.

Incidentally, we're purposely omitting consideration of the 1983-84 models built by the "New Avanti Motor Corporation" headed by Stephen Blake. As the accompanying story points out, these cars have been substantially revised from the last Avanti IIs and, though they will no doubt be highly prized in the future, it's simply too early to assess their position in the market with any precision.

As shown on the value chart (see sidebar), the early Studebaker models command higher prices in any condition class than Avanti IIs, reflecting their more limited production and unique status as first of the line. The most desirable cars in this group are those with the optional R2 or R3 engines. Because of their rarity, they customarily bring 10-15 percent more than the basic R1-equipped models in comparable condition. Other extras to look for are those that add to the value of any car, such as air conditioning, radio, limited-slip differential, special interior, and so on.

Regardless of tune, only one engine was used in the Studebaker Avantis, the familiar 289-cid V-8. Although quite antiquated even by early-'60s standards (its basic engineering harked back to 1951), this mill was still capable of delivering good performance, reasonable fuel economy, and long-lived service. Its big bugaboo is its well-known habit of leaking and burning oil, but it's basically trouble-free provided you pay attention to the sump level. Transmissions, whether manual or automatic, were Borg-Warner components, and are also judged reliable.

Parts availability for early Avantis is quite good today. This is due in large measure to continued production as the Avanti II, of course, and a good many items are still available from Nate Altman's parts operation in South Bend. The cars also enjoy strong club support from

---

Clubs for Avanti Owners

Avanti Owners Association
7840 Michelle Drive
La Mesa, CA 92041

Avanti Owners Association International
P.O. Box 322
Uxbridge, MA 01569

Studebaker Automobile Club of America
P.O. Box 5036
Hemet, CA 92343

Studebaker Drivers Club
P.O. Box 3044
South Bend, IN 46619

---

the Avanti Owners Association, the Avanti Owners Association International, and the Studebaker Drivers' Club. One snag is replacement factory upholstery material, which is now difficult to come by, though this will only trouble those concerned with an original, 100-point restoration.

The early Avanti's main drawback as a collectible is fit and finish, which was indifferent at best, reflecting Studebaker president Sherwood Egbert's production hurry-up and the related fiberglass molding problems on the earliest bodies. No doubt most of the build bugs have long since been exterminated on restored examples, but it's something to keep in mind if you're considering an unrestored car. Also keep in mind that while the Avanti's body won't rust—one of the few Studebakers so blessed—its chassis can because it's steel, just like a Corvette's. Because it was intended mainly as a high-performance machine, the early Avanti invited hard driving, so your condition check should include careful inspection of steering, brakes, springs, shocks, and differential for signs of undue wear and possible abuse.

The Avanti II's chief attraction is that it combines the striking original style with greater luxury and, up through 1975 at least, superior workmanship. Some enthusiasts prefer the II for this reason even though it is less "pure" (i.e., not all-Studebaker) and has slightly lower performance. Offsetting this is the switch to Chevrolet running gear, which makes the II a much more practical proposition for those who'd rather enjoy their cars on the road and not just on the judging stand. The 327-cid V-8 used through 1969 is revvier and freer-running than the detoxed 350, and though the latter is still in current production (in modified form as the L-84 "Cross Fire" Corvette unit) it offers no real advantage over the earlier engine in parts supplies or costs.

As noted, Avanti II workmanship deteriorated in the years following Nate Altman's death (especially paint, body, and chrome finish), as did gas mileage under the weight of required safety add-ons and more strangling emissions controls. Also as the '70s progressed, Avanti's solutions to meeting some requirements became increasingly of the afterthought variety, notable in such areas as haphazard minor controls and jury-rigged air conditioning installations. Therefore, we'd recommend the 1965-69 models as your best all-around choices in this group, followed by the 1970-75s and the 1976-82s in that order.

One final, rather esoteric point about the Avanti II concerns restoration. While most cars left the South Bend plant with a fairly limited number of paint colors and interior trim materials, a small percentage were built to customer order with some very specific—and, in some cases, very bizarre—equipment. Such a car would present obvious restoration problems for those concerned with preserving it in its original state. The flip side of this is that one need be relatively *less* concerned about authenticity with an Avanti II restoration precisely because so few cars were built the same way. This opens up the inviting prospect of being able to update the car with more modern equipment than originally installed without detracting from the car's individualized, hand-built aura. In fact, this is exactly what Altman set out to do—introduce newer components as they became available to keep the car "current"—and it's what Steve Blake is doing with the latest Avantis. Few collector cars offer such freedom of expression. And that's appropriate, because that's what the Avanti has always been about.

The Collectible Avanti: Value Guide

1963-64 Studebaker Avanti
Restorable: $3000-$4500
Good: $3500-$8000
Excellent: $8000-$14,000
Add 10% for 1964 models.
Add 10-15% for R-series engines.
5-year projection: +75%

1965-82 Avanti II
Restorable: $2500-$3500
Good: $3500-$7000
Excellent: $7000-$12,000
5-year projection: +25%

What's It Worth? Should I Keep It?
Which Cars Make the Best Investments?

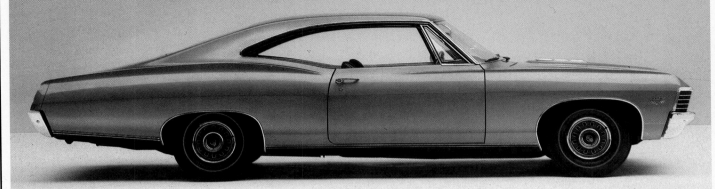

The Complete Book of Collectible Cars 1940-1980 has the answers. Over 600 blue-chip old-car buys!

Here's an investment than can pay big dividends: *The Complete Book of Collectible Cars 1940-1980,* an authoritative guide to the "classics" and the "comers" among post-war automobiles. It covers 600 foreign and domestic cars that have high interest value today and high profit potential tomorrow.

Each blue-chip collectible profile highlights model design origins, over-the-road performance, and production and sales figures. Entries also include brief specifications, original list prices, and unique "For" and "Against" collectibility factors. Realistic price ranges are also provided plus a percentage estimate of collector value five years down the road. *The Complete Book of Collectible Cars 1940-1980* is an investment guide that will help you "drive all the way to the bank."

384 pages with 32 pages in 4-color

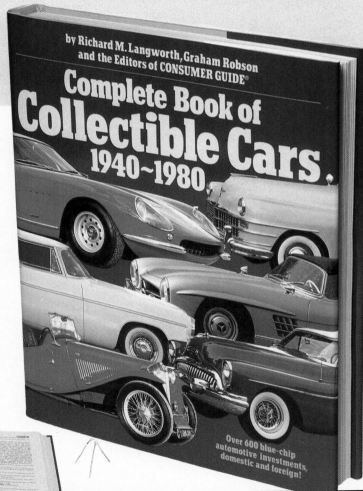

Available in bookstores or order directly from the publisher by sending $14.98 plus $1.95 for shipping and handling (Illinois residents add 6% sales tax) to:

PUBLICATIONS INTERNATIONAL, LTD.
3841 W. Oakton Street
Skokie, Illinois 60076

BMW 507:
Germany's Improbable Sports Car

by Eric Dahlquist

Europe had been warm in the early summer of 1972. Carolyn Dahlquist and I had gone to France to see the Citroën GS plant at Renne and then to Modena in Italy to savor the new mid-engine V-8 Maserati Bora and V-6 Merak. At that time, Citroën was running Maserati. Later, I would move on to Daimler-Benz in Stuttgart to drive the heroic W154 and W196 Grand Prix cars—an adventure few, if any, writers would ever again experience, these mighty racers having become priceless antiques. An hour to the south by air lay Munich, the "Paris of Germany," where the 1972 Summer Olympics would be held in October. Although no one could know it as June turned into July, the Games would be rocked by the fanatical mission of a handful of Arab terrorists. Fortunately for us, we would be an ocean and a continent away when that happened.

I had been to Munich before, running full tilt down the smooth, wide *autobahnen*, exploring the glorious Bavarian countryside and falling in love with its people and their beloved BMWs. One car in particular had caught my eye on two previous visits. It was lined up with other of the firm's automotive landmarks in the old BMW Museum. A few of the "art deco" BMWs like the 327 coupe and 335 cabriolet were vaguely familiar to me from early-Fifties foreign films of wartorn Germany. Though the images were slightly faded, these once-hot, once-stylish automobiles flitted in and out of those black-and-white scenes like ghosts from the lost German dream. Even so, one could still sense the powerful atmosphere in which they were created.

But it was the Type 507 that had really attracted my attention. It was an expression not of past epochs but of the phoenix-like German industrial miracle that began gathering speed in the 1950s. The 507 is also a perfect example of the keen foresight of Max Hoffman, the man who, more than any other, was responsible for the European import car boom in America.

World War II altered the destiny of millions, and Hoffman had been affected as much as anyone. A Rolls-Royce and Bentley dealer in 1930s Austria, he realized as soon as the Continent began gearing for war that there would soon be little demand for luxury automobiles, especially British

It was a most unlikely product for a firm struggling in the aftermath of World War II: a costly V-8-powered sports car. But the timelessly styled 507 reaffirmed BMW's standing as a builder of truly sporting machines —and in no uncertain terms.

Opposite page: A mountain scene makes an appropriate backdrop for James L. Roman's flawlessly restored Bavarian stormer—only these are the mountains of Colorado, not Germany. This page, top: The 507's folding top was quite well integrated with the taut, muscular body lines. Above: What a place for two lucky people on a sunny, top-down day! Note shifter location and floor-mount seats. Left: All-aluminum 507 V-8 is a lovely sight, not all that different from current BMW sixes.

Being the astute market analyst he was, Max Hoffman knew the U.S. would go for a sports car with svelte styling, German solidity, and something anyone could relate to: a V-8.

Above: Factory phantom view reveals the 507's thorough engineering. The two-seater was built on a short-wheelbase (97.6-inch) version of the capable Type 501/502 sedan platform. Opposite page: Even with plain wheels the 507 looks striking.

ones. So he sold out and left Europe for America, where he started a plastics factory in 1941. It incorporated a novel metalization process needed for the burgeoning U.S. war effort, and his business prospered for the duration.

When peace returned, Hoffman decided to get back into the import-car business—to the utter amazement of his friends and associates. He knew that the U.S. market was wide open in the postwar period for the kind of super-luxury sports cars and sports sedans Europe was long famous for. Moreover, he knew that America was about the only outlet for such products aside from Switzerland. The demand might not be in the six-digit numbers Detroit uses to measure success, but it would be high enough to make Hoffman one of the wealthiest auto entrepreneurs in the world. During its heyday, his import empire owned the distribution rights for, or had some hand in selling, almost every major European make that ever

landed on the East Coast. And if you lived in New York City and wanted to know what was happening car-wise overseas, all you had to do was visit Maxie's showroom.

Hoffman had always loved BMWs. One evening at his exquisite country house in Austria he related to me how it started. As a young man he had been a champion bicycle racer. Later he graduated to motorcycles, which he rode for a short time. In 1923, BMW introduced its cross-mounted horizontally opposed motorcycle engine with universal shaft drive, and its bikes became the ones to race—and beat—in European competition. As a former racer, Hoffman could appreciate the firm's engineering skill and innovation. When BMW began producing cars in 1929, Hoffman realized this motorcycle maker would inevitably be a force in the auto industry—much the way Honda would be decades later.

All of which brings us to 1953-54. BMW had been revived after the war,

but its fortunes were slipping now due to the very resurgence in the German economy it was helping to stimulate. Four wheels had become more desirable than two in the first glimmer of a re-emerging European affluence, but the partition of Germany had left BMW only "half a company" and most of its car-building operations had been lost behind the Iron Curtain.

By 1952, however, the firm had sufficiently recovered to re-enter the car business, and introduced its first postwar model, the florid Type 501 sedan. It was nicknamed the "Baroque Angel" because of its bulky, curvaceous lines. A few years later, BMW would enter the opposite end of the market with the Isetta "egg car," one of the most original (some say funny) economy cars of all time. But for now it was more expeditious to field this *luxus* sedan, carefully engineered and finely crafted. Trouble was, it could only be built in small numbers owing to lack of production facilities, and the resulting high price made it all but unobtainable for most Germans.

In America, Max Hoffman began importing 501s while noting the nation's growing interest in sports cars. Detroit seemed interested, too. Nash had been the first major domestic maker to try one, fielding the Anglo-American Nash-Healey for 1951. Soon, Chevrolet had its Corvette, Kaiser introduced its Darrin in a last-gasp effort to win back customers, and Ford was on the verge of debuting the Thunderbird. In Europe, BMW's perennial rival in Swabia was about to launch a superbly designed supercar for the super rich derived from its 300SL racers of 1952. With its sleek coupe bodywork featuring unusual "gullwing" doors plus a lusty 3.0-liter ohc six for power, the production 300SL caused a quiet riot when it was displayed in prototype form at the 1954 New York Auto Show.

Hoffman had persuaded Daimler-Benz to produce the roadgoing 300SL, one of the first European cars designed with the U.S. market in mind. Later, he would be the instigator of the 190SL, D-B's sports car for the "masses." But being the astute market analyst he was, Hoffman saw the 300SL as too "rich" and rare for middle-class Yankees, and lower-priced British roadsters like the Triumph TR2 were too anemic and crude. Further, Detroit's new two-seaters were all somehow pretenders in his mind, deficient in performance, handling, styling, and craftsmanship. What he thought the U.S. would really go for was a true sports car combining svelte looks with the kind of solidity only the Germans could build, plus the one feature any American could relate to, a V-8.

Of course,, Hoffman knew that BMW already had such a car—cleverly concealed as the 501. And in mid-1954, Munich made things more interesting by slotting in a newly developed 2.6 liter all-aluminum V-8 to create the Type 502. All that remained to be done was to design an appropriately beautiful body and drop it on the sedan chassis— the same approach, incidentally, that would produce the 190SL.

BMW management had reached many of the same conclusions. The idea of using the 501/502 platform as the basis for a sporting car was first broached in 1954, and Munich's long-time chief engineer Fritz Fiedler had commissioned a prototype from the Bauer coachworks in Stuttgart. Ultimately this led to the Type 503, a close-coupled coupe and cabriolet bowing at the Frankfurt *Automobil-Ausstellung* in September 1955. Powered by a 3.2-liter enlargement of the V-8, also used in the 3.2 version of the 501/502, the 503 had 140 bhp at its disposal. Bodywork was done in light alloy over the 111.6-inch sedan chassis, and the novel suspension with torsion bars all-round, double A-arm front geometry and live rear axle was retained. The 503's outer panels were little more than a "skin" covering a sturdy all-steel inner body welded rigidly to the massive square-tube sedan frame, and because of this they were hardly any lighter than the "Angels." They were sporting cars certainly, but scarcely sports cars.

It was here that Maxie Hoffman again played instigator. Though there are several stories of how the Type 507 came to be, all seem to connect Hoffman with the young industrial designer who had styled the 503, with the initial contact occurring sometime in early 1954, probably at the same New York Auto Show where the 300SL premiered. That young designer was Albrecht Goertz, who up until

Opposite page, top: Accessory hardtop nicely complemented the 507's handsome lines. It's a rare find today on this very low-volume sports car. Bottom: Also styled by Albrecht Goertz, the four-seat Type 503 (cabriolet shown) debuted alongside the 507 in late 1955. Right: Photographed in Colorado Springs in 1983, this fully restored 507 is the prize possession of James L. Roman.

then had had virtually no experience in the auto business. Goertz recently related that Hoffman was at the show and saw some sketches of a new sports car BMW was working on, though it's unclear whether this was the forthcoming 503 or something completely different. What is clear is that Hoffman didn't like it. He also felt strongly that the kind of dour, traditionally Teutonic styling embodied in the "Baroque Angel" wouldn't even get a second glance on Park Avenue or Sunset Boulevard—which is where it counted in this league. So, according to the designer, Hoffman urged Goertz to submit ideas for a two-seater. He did, the powers in Munich were intrigued, and Goertz had the assignment by November.

Also clear is engineer Fiedler's eagerness to move Heaven and Earth—and radiators and carburetors—to make the mechanical package fit Goertz's lines. Goertz had lately left the employ of Raymond Loewy, whose team at Studebaker had created the daring Starliner/Starlight coupes of 1953. Perhaps it's not surprising then that the finished 507 displayed some of the same themes, especially the classic long-hood/short-deck proportions, large wheel well openings, and swooping fender lines. But where the Studebakers were obviously tailored to fit American marketing requirements, the 507 remained more faithful to Goertz's original ideas, and it emerged taut, lean, and simple, with only a few concessions to the sales department. It debuted alongside the 503 at Frankfurt in 1955—and naturally put its stablemates in the shade. It was a critical success, acclaimed on both sides of the Atlantic as a near ideal expression of the automotive art.

In Hoffman's view, the 507's commercial success hinged on a selling price of around $5000 and production of at least 5000 units annually. It didn't

quite work out that way. Production began very slowly, and it was a full two years before the first 507s landed in New York. By that time the price had escalated to $9000—and there still weren't that many cars available. In later years Hoffman admitted that, at the time, he thought the scenario could play out this way, but he pushed the project nonetheless, feeling BMW's image needed all the help it could get in the U.S. That was especially true after 1955 and introduction of the Isetta.

"If" is a qualifier that usually crops up in near-miss automotive ventures, and it crops up here. You see, if the 507 could have been built in reasonable quantity in 1956-57 and if price could have been held to around $5000, this car would have been a Corvette and Thunderbird killer. Its V-8 was tuned to deliver 150 DIN horsepower, about 170 SAE, and with a 2800-pound curb weight the 507 was capable of 7.0-second 0-60 mph sprints. Top speed was an honest 128 mph with a 3.7:1 rear axle ratio, and 138 mph was available with a 3.42:1 gearset and an even more potent 160-bhp (DIN) engine tune. Even modified Corvettes of the period were pressed for numbers like these, let alone being able to sail along at 24 mpg at a steady 60 mph.

This story was pieced together from conversations with various factory personnel and Max Hoffman between 1969, when I first saw a 507 in the old BMW Museum, and that summer of '72, when I finally got a chance to drive one. I had made arrangements by letter, and the car was made ready by museum director Gunter Kiehl, who would accompany me on a day-long excursion. Kiehl, a terrific car enthusiast, had lately come to BMW after setting up the renowned Daimler-Benz corporate museum, and he was looking forward to this trip as much as I was.

It seemed somehow strangely appropriate that our 507 would be the very one Pvt. Elvis Presley had used during his tour of duty in Germany. One might wonder whether any American, even a rock star, would consider this more like Detroit iron instead of a European car. The 507 was certainly as easy to drive as any U.S. car. The 3.2-liter/193-cid engine is docile even at low revs, and shines with many of the same virtues that have endeared V-8s to Yankee hearts for some three generations now. Looking into the wide engine compartment, I found myself mentally comparing the handsome BMW engine to its Studebaker contemporary.

Sliding behind the wheel, though, I

The 507's split grille can be thought of as preserving BMW's trademark "twin-kidney" motif, but in a horizontal format.
Car shown top owned by Gil Steward.

found myself thinking more about the '55 T-Bird and Corvette. All three have the same close-to-the-floor driving stance, where you have to stretch your legs straight out to reach the pedals. Compared to the starship-like digital instruments of the Eighties, the 507's large, round analog speedometer and tachometer might seem primitive, but the dash layout was state-of-the-art for the late Fifties and it still looks good and works well.

Because of its all-aluminum con-struction, the BMW V-8 has a differ-ent character compared to the typical cast-iron Detroit mill, broadcasting a unique, far-away kind of "alloy sound" that gives the impression of light metal parts whirring with great purpose. Our drive route took us over a variety of roads, from the deliciously fast *autobahnen* to the intricate one-lane paved roller coasters that run like black asphalt ribbons across rural Ba-varia. At one point a then-new BMW 2002 tii sedan gave chase. Despite its more advanced age the 507 was well up to the challenge, and could run at equal—and high—velocities over most of the secondary roads, which

says a lot for its live-axle rear sus-pension and the lustiness of that engine.

With its nearly equal 50/50 weight distribution, the 507 has great over-steering ability just like a race car. You can hang the tail out a mile with only the slightest variations in pressure on the sensitive throttle. By contrast, the ride seems almost "trucky," though it's not harsh. The tubular chassis con-fers high torsional rigidity in this open roadster and there is virtually no cowl shake or rattling even on rippled roads. The rack-and-pinion steering is very light—twitchy by today's stan-dards. Conversely, the shift action on the four-speed gearbox, while lacking the butter-smoothness of current BMW linkages, is still impressive and a cut above that on many of today's cars. Throws are easy, precise, and short.

After a day behind the wheel, yank-ing the car swiftly through tight switchback curves and along hump-backed roads, it's easy to come away feeling that the 507 is one of the hap-piest automotive combinations ever. It remains a surprisingly modern car despite the technological advances made in the years since it appeared. In particular, it's pleasingly well-balanced, an artful blend of per-formance, roadability, refinement, comfort and, of course, that gorgeous styling. There are few more recent designs that succeed so well in so many ways.

I am told that a 100-point 507 was recently sold to the Henry Ford Mu-seum in Dearborn for close to $55,000. Personally, I don't think it's worth that much—except maybe to a museum. It's a wonderful automobile, maybe even a great automobile, but for me it lacks the visceral excitement of the 300SL Gullwing—and most of all its formidable racing heritage. In terms of driving pleasure the 507 is far su-perior to the 289 and 427 Cobra but, again, the gut appeal of an unrivalled competition legacy will always add to the Cobra's perceived value for some enthusiasts.

In a way, the BMW 507 is like those people we often hear about who enjoy moderate success in life but never make it really big. A certain element of luck is usually involved in the making of any superstar, and luck was not on the side of the 507. Too bad. It deserved better.

BMW 507: Collector's Notes

The BMW 507 has had an impact all out of proportion to its numbers or its commercial value to the company. Some say BMW lost money on every one it sold; others say just the reverse. Regardless, only 254 chassis are known to have been built. All but three of these were fitted with "production" bodywork, although every 507 is, in a sense, a "custom" job because of hand labor variations from one to the next and because mechanical components were changed on an as-needed basis. As for the other three chassis, one was the prototype designed by Goertz, one was rebodied by Raymond Loewy in a style predictive of his future Avanti design, and one received a Vignale body built by Scaglietti.

This rarity makes all 507s worth restoring no matter what their original condition. The $55,000 paid by the Ford Museum is the highest price for a 507 I know of, but it's possible—though not very likely—to find one needing total or partial restoration for a good deal less. Restoration won't be easy, of course, for the reasons already mentioned. And this is hardly the sort of car you run across every day.

Estimates vary widely on the number of survivors. In 1975 a longtime 507 owner, John Kessler of Richmond, Virginia, compiled a register listing some 180 examples, but the German BMW Vintage Club has more recently accounted for about 200. Currently, the BMW Vintage Club of America is attempting to update the 507 register. Inquiries should be directed to Richard Neville, 148 Linden Street, Suite 302, Wellseley, MA 02181.

The largest BMW club in the U.S. is the BMW Car Club of America, founded in 1968 and currently numbering 13,000 members. Its address is 345 Harvard Street, Cambridge, MA 02138. The BMW 507 Club USA is open to owners of any of Munich's V-8 models and, unusually, charges no dues. Its address is Hilltown Pike, Hilltown, PA 18927.

I have owned a 507 for some 12 years and have found it a most satisfactory car in every respect. My car still wears its original paint, though its upholstery and top have been replaced. Incidentally, the top can be raised or lowered almost with one hand and looks good either way. BMW also offered an accessory hardtop, a rare item and a real find today, that did nothing to detract from the car's sleek looks. But there's a lot more to the 507 than its "pretty face"—as you'll discover if you're ever lucky enough to get the chance to drive one.

—*Gilbert L. Steward, Jr.*

The Car Spotter

This 1956 Studebaker President Classic was spotted recently at a used car lot/garage in Castle Rock, Colorado. The special rocker panel molding distinguishes Classic models from regular Presidents, and the Classic rode a four-inch-longer wheelbase. While this example's interior was very rough, the body was nearly perfect. Best of all, it was equipped with factory air.

Cars With Personalities
BY JOHN A. CONDE

This 248-page book features a marvelous collection of 573 contemporary photographs of automobiles with famous people from all walks of life, from 1896 to the present . . . hundreds of Packards, Cadillacs, Cords, Duesenbergs, Pierce-Arrows, Mercedes, Lincolns, and other great motorcars of the classic past . . . 122 different car makes represented, with film stars, aviation and automotive pioneers, political leaders, radio and Broadway luminaries, inventors, band leaders, opera singers, and more. JOHN A. CONDE, whose first book _The Cars That Hudson Built_ was published in 1980, is a noted automotive historian and writer recognized for his broad interest in the development of the automobile industry. After spending 32 years with American Motors, he was named curator of transportation at the Henry Ford Museum in 1977. He retired recently to devote full time to writing and lecturing on automobile history.

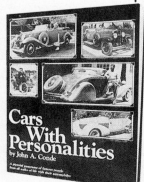

General John J. Pershing with his Cadillac staff car during World War I

USE THIS FORM TO ORDER NOW ✓ **$21.95 POSTPAID**

☑ My check or money order for $21.95 is enclosed. ☑ Charge to my account.

Thomas Gipple 50

MY VISA OR MASTER CARD NO.   EXPIRATION DATE

SIGNED 52 BARNACLE - LN

(REQUIRED ONLY IF YOU AUTHORIZE A CHARGE.)

PLEASE SEND THE HARDBOUND BOOK
CARS WITH PERSONALITIES TO:

NAME LUSBY MARYLAND 20657

STREET FIRE ESAPE PION

CITY 410-586-23 STATE 22   ZIP

Make remittance payable to: ARNOLD-PORTER PUBLISHING CO. and mail to Box 646, Keego Harbor, Michigan 48033.

Telephone orders also accepted. Call 313-338-4478 anytime from 9 A.M. to 10 P.M. _Michigan residents add 88¢ sales tax._

More great issues of Collectible Automobile are on the way!
Here's your chance to enjoy the best for less!

This is the one that sets a new standard of excellence for old-car hobby periodicals. Every issue of Collectible Automobile brings you page after page of gorgeous color photography and lively, informative feature articles prepared by the most respected names in the field. And nowhere else will you find such provocative yet useful features as Cheap Wheels, Future Collectibles, Collectible Scale Automobile, or the easiest to use guide to collector car values ever created. No doubt about it: Collectible Automobile is a premium-quality package that puts the accent on class. Quite simply, it's the best magazine of its kind. Isn't it time you treated yourself to the best?

Don't miss a single issue! Subscribe now to Collectible Automobile and take advantage of special low rates!

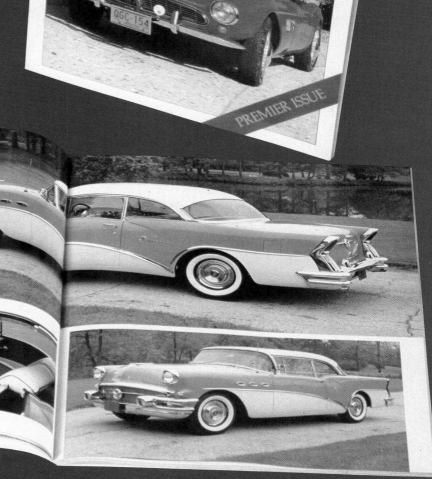

Don't wait! Fill out and mail the order card today!

The American Hardtop: Convertibles That Didn't Convert (and one that did)

by Joseph H. Wherry

It was a simple idea, really: just a closed car without the usual fixed center roof pillar. But greatness often comes from simplicity, and today the American hardtop must be considered one of the most significant design developments in automotive history. It was certainly the single most popular body style of the post-war era.

General Motors got the ball rolling, as everyone knows, by introducing the first volume-production hardtops for 1949. Just three years later, every Detroit nameplate save Kaiser-Frazer had fielded at least one, usually with the best trim and equipment in the catalog. Soon, hardtops were appearing in lower-line series, then with four doors, then as station wagons. The idea was so popular that ordinary coupes and sedans began acquiring thin-pillar "hardtop styling," and normally conservative Cadillac turned all its closed models (except

limousines) into hardtops for 1959. A few foreign manufacturers like Rootes in England got into the act. By 1960, the hardtop had far outpaced the true convertible in U.S. production, and in most years from then until the early '70s it would be second in sales only to that traditional favorite, the four-door sedan.

Though the hardtop phenomenon began in the years right after World War II, its origins actually go back to World War I. Up to this time, automobile bodies had pretty much followed the styles and construction methods laid down by the makers of horse-drawn carriages. This meant both open and closed types built up from a wooden structural framework overlaid with wood or fabric panels. The open touring and roadster bodies were far more common than closed styles in these years. They were cheaper to build and thus sold for less, and many motorists preferred

their "outdoorsy" feel, though their flimsy folding canopies and clumsy side curtains weren't the best for foul-weather comfort. Coupes and sedans of this era did not have hard tops but rather fabric-covered roofs. And, though intricately framed, these were scarcely any sturdier than folding tops. Some people objected to the doorposts on closed models as hindrances to getting in or out, and to the vertical sliding windows that tended to loosen in their tracks over time.

Then came two developments that enhanced the closed car's appeal. One was the advent of mass production by Henry Ford with his Model T, which would make closed cars comparable in price with open models. The second was the introduction of all-steel bodies by the Dodge Brothers in November 1914. (Horace and John Dodge were experts in steel fabrication techniques.) Testimony to steel's greater ruggedness came

Wherry

quickly from no less than General John J. Pershing, whose Dodge staff cars served with distinction—and considerable publicity—as part of his expeditionary force in Mexico against Pancho Villa.

Just two years later, 1916, the Dodges introduced a coupe with removable doorposts. This not only answered an objection to closed bodywork but also created the first "hardtop convertible." When not needed to provide location for the two plate-glass windows on each side, the posts stowed conveniently in the trunk. This design seemed to offer the best of both worlds. The steel top was sturdier than flapping canvas on a spindly frame that could collapse in a driving wind or under heavy snow, yet occupants still had that "out-of-doors" feeling.

Not surprisingly, accessory manufacturers and other automakers were quick to copy. The 1920 Velie four-seat

Opposite page: Chrysler created the first postwar hardtop with its 1946 Town & Country prototype. Only seven were built. This page, top: Photographer Bud Juneau is the owner of this pioneering 1949 Buick Roadmaster Riviera. Production was low, just 4343 units. Above: Removable doorposts made this 1916 Dodge Brothers three-passenger coupe the first true hardtop-convertible. Style inspired the "California Top" of the Twenties.

In the early postwar years it seemed the public couldn't get enough of hardtops, and Detroit scrambled to meet demand. By 1952, all the majors except Kaiser-Frazer had at least one.

sports model coupled prophetic "hardtop styling" with external exhaust pipes. The Stephens, made in Freeport, Illinois, was offered with a snazzy pillarless top featuring rear portholes, an ancestor of the 1956 Thunderbird top, and the 1920-22 Carroll had an even more modern-looking design.

Then came detachable "hard" tops, many stronger than even the sedan roofs of the day. The best-known was the "California Top," which soon became the rage for all sorts of cars in the Twenties. These well-built roofs, usually steel covered with genuine patent leather, were the forerunners of the lift-off hardtops that appeared as accessories for a number of sports cars in the mid-'50s and remain popular today. They were, more than anything else, a styling concession to

those who wanted a convertible's open-air flavor plus the snugness of a closed car and didn't care whether the top folded away or not.

The next logical step was a hardtop-convertible that actually *did* convert, with a metal top that could be stowed within the bodywork. As with so many of today's innovations, this one came from overseas—but it appeared fully two decades before Ford's 1957

Opposite page, top and far left: Peugeot's 1936 Eclipse was the forerunner of the retractable hardtop-convertible. Ford's Skyliner "retrac" of 1957-59 used a similar top stowage arrangement, but needed three motors to the French car's one. This page, top: Oldsmobile's Futuramic 98 Holiday was one of the three pace-setting 1949 GM models. Production was 3006 units. Owner: Woody Hyde. Left: Show car and hardtop styling combined in the 1954 Buick Super Riviera, one of four hardtops offered by the division that year. Super production was 73,531. Above: Ford added a new twist to the hardtop idea with its 1954 Crestline Skyliner. Priced about $110 above the standard Victioria two-door, it featured a forward roof section made of green-tinted Plexiglas. The public didn't take well to the idea, and production totalled only 13,344.

Skyliner "retrac." It was the sleek two/four-seat Peugeot Eclipse, built on the Type 601 chassis and introduced by the venerable French firm in *1936*! Its steel top slid neatly away under a "trunklid" hinged at the rear and raised at its forward edge by two curved arms. It's fascinating to wonder whether Dearborn's designers studied the Eclipse, because this description also fits the Skyliner. One

difference: Peugeot managed to stash the top with just one electric motor instead of three.

Though General Motors gets credit for the first volume-production American hardtops, Chrysler gets credit for the first of the postwar breed. This was one of the wood-bodied Town & Country models proposed for 1946 but withdrawn from consideration after seven prototypes

were built (see "Town & Country: Rare Elegance" in this issue). It's a pity the company got cold feet, because the T&C hardtop caused quite a stir and undoubtedly would have sold handsomely.

Thus, it was left to GM to pioneer the American hardtop—which it did, in characteristic fashion, by simply overwhelming the market. It launched not one but three pillarless

69

coupes—the Buick Roadmaster Riviera, the Cadillac Series 62 Coupe deVille, and the Oldsmobile Futuramic 98 Holiday—all at mid-model year 1949. All were stunningly successful, the Cadillac in particular, which sold at about twice the rate of its siblings as a proportion of overall division output. The race was on.

Over the next few years it seemed as if the public couldn't get enough of the hardtop idea, and Detroit scrambled to meet demand. GM upped the ante the next year by introducing the Bel Air in the Chevrolet Deluxe line and no fewer than four Pontiac Chieftain Catalina models (six and V-8, Deluxe and Super). All these had been planned for 1949, but various corporate decisions forced the one-year delay. Chrysler chimed in for 1950 with entries from three of its divisions: the Dodge Coronet Diplomat, the DeSoto Custom Sportsman, and three Chrysler Newport hardtops, a Windsor, a New Yorker and a Town & Country.

The ranks swelled again for '51. Ford bowed its new Victoria in the V-8 Custom series after having made do the previous season with a flashy two-door sedan, the interesting Crestliner. Plymouth completed Chrysler's commitment with the Cranbrook Belvedere. The independents also got in

the game this year. Nash contributed a Country Club hardtop version of its compact Rambler, Hudson added Hollywood hardtops to all four of its model lines, and Packard released its pretty Mayfair in the low-end "250" group. Chrysler, not forgetting luxury-car buyers, fielded still another Newport, this time wearing the Imperial badge.

Model year 1952 saw more entries from Dearborn in the Lincoln Cosmopolitan Capri and Mercury's new Monterey. Nash, whose senior cars were likewise totally redesigned, took the opportunity to offer Country Club hardtops in both Ambassador and Statesman trim. Studebaker, then in the last year of its pacesetting 1947 body design, produced two Starliner hardtops in the Champion Regal and Commander State series. Little Wil-

Right: GM got a jump on the rest of the industry in mid-1955 with pillarless four-doors at Buick and Oldsmobile. Shown is that year's Olds Super 88 Holiday Sedan. Production was 47,385. Owner: Terry McElfresh. Below: Ford's jazzy 1955 Fairlane Crown Victoria was an attempt at combining hardtop looks with the rigidity of a standard sedan. A Plexi-top version was offered in addition to the steel-roof model shown here. Production was 33,165 and 1999, respectively. Opposite page, bottom: Cadillac built 24,086 of its Coupe de Ville for 1956. Owner: Larry Schaal.

lys, a fast-sinking contender in the market, nonetheless managed to come up with one of the prettiest of the lot, the Aero-Eagle. Packard, harking back to Ford's earlier limited-edition sedans, produced the Sportster in its junior Clipper line. This hardtop-styled pillared two-door would be one of Packard's rarest postwar production models.

A new high in styling class appeared for 1953 from an unlikely source: the all-new, very European-looking Starliner hardtop from Studebaker. Offered in both Champion and Commander guise and styled by Raymond Loewy, it remains, in the opinion of many critics, the most outstanding U.S. automotive design of the postwar era. Other than this notable achievement, no other new hardtops appeared that year.

The Loewy coupes returned mostly unadulterated for 1954, a year that also brought us the ancestor of today's moonroof in the Ford Crestline Skyliner and the Mercury Monterey Sun Valley. Both these cars were distinguished by their unusual see-through forward roof sections of green-tinted Plexiglas. Neither sold well, largely because of excessive cabin heat and an interior ambience not unlike that of the Emerald City of Oz, but they were interesting attempts at new variations on the hardtop theme.

A more successful one was the hardtop with four doors. Another GM innovation, it appeared initially during 1955 as the Riviera sedan in the Buick Special and Century series and as Holiday sedans in all three Oldsmobile series. Packard added the awkwardly named Clipper Custom Constellation and a senior Four Hundred hardtop. Ford again tried to be different with the Crown Victoria in its new top-line Fairlane series, a jazzy pillared two-door with a wide wrapover roof molding that extended down to cover the B-posts. The "Crown Vicky" didn't sell nearly as well as the regular Victoria hardtop, and the Plexi-roof version found only about 2000 customers. Wagons also came in for hardtop styling inspiration this year as GM translated one of Harley Earl's show car designs into the production Chevrolet Bel Air Nomad and Pontiac Star Chief Safari, both two-doors. Performance fans looked to Chrysler this year and its new 300 hardtop, a beautiful blend of

By the mid-Fifties, hardtops were outselling all other body styles except the four-door sedan, and had become a permanent part of new-model planning in Detroit.

Above: The 1955 Chrysler C300 hardtop coupe. Right: The 1957 Chrysler New Yorker hardtop coupe. Owner: Carl Bilter. Below: Chevrolet's Bel Air Sport Coupe for 1957. Owner: Bill Bodnarchuk. Opposite page, top: The 1957 Cadillac Series 62 Sedan de Ville. Owner: Vicky Bach. Bottom left: The 1956 Rambler Custom Country Club hardtop sedan. Bottom right: Mercury's glitzy Turnpike Cruiser hardtop sedan for 1957 (production prototype).

Wherry

the "100 Million Dollar Look" with an Imperial grille and the most powerful engine yet seen from Detroit, the famed hemi V-8 packing 300 bhp.

Four-door hardtops blossomed for 1956, with entries from each of the Big Three plus Rambler. The latter also offered a genuine "hardtop wagon" sans center posts as the Custom and Super Cross Country. Chrysler released a squadron of high-performance hardtops as companions to the 300, the Plymouth Fury and the DeSoto Fireflite Adventurer, and the D-500 option at Dodge was available for any model, including the hardtops. The year also saw the debut of the unbelievably priced ($10,000) Continental Mark II hardtop and a handsome facelift from Studebaker that created the Golden Hawk and Sky Hawk.

Hardtop highlights for '57 included new pillarless wagons from Buick and Olds (called Caballero and Fiesta, respectively), the last Nash and Hud-

son models of all kinds, the glitzy Mercury Turnpike Cruiser two- and four-door hardtops, the fascinatingly complex Ford Skyliner retractable already mentioned, and the first V-8 Rambler, the limited-production Custom Rebel four-door. Not to be overlooked is the Cadillac Eldorado Brougham, a hardtop sedan with rear-hinged back doors, a price even higher than the Mark II's ($13,000), and full-house standard equipment that included a matched set of silver drinking tumblers, a makeup kit, and air suspension.

By now, the hardtop idea was a permanent part of new-model planning in Detroit. The examples we've listed so far are all quite collectible, but there would be more memorable hardtops in the ensuing 15 years. Examples are the various Edsels, the 1958 Packard Hawk and the Studebaker-based standard hardtop, the four-door hardtop wagons of the

early '60s from Chrysler and Dodge, full-size "buckets-and-console" cars like the Buick Invicta Wildcat and Pontiac Grand Prix (both new for '62), hardtop versions of the hot mid-size muscle cars like the Pontiac GTO, pillarless ponycars like the 1967-68 Mercury Cougar XR-7, and personal-luxury models like the front-drive 1966 Olds Toronado. The list is almost endless.

Hardtops have virtually disappeared nowadays. Ironically it was GM that abandoned them first, in 1973, partly in anticipation of a government standard for roof strength in a rollover situation, a mandate that was never enacted. But as the leader goes, so go the others, and by 1980 there wasn't a single American hardtop left in production. One wonders whether Detroit will see fit to revive the hardtop in the same way it's now rushing back to convertibles. For our part, we sure hope so.

Ironically, the company that had pioneered the American hardtop was the first to abandon it. The ostensible reason was a proposed government rule.

Opposite page, top: The ultra-pricey Continental Mark II, 1956. Lower left: One of the last Packards was this '58 hardtop. Lower right: Ford's Fairlane 500 Skyliner for '58. This page, top: Chevy's 1962 Bel Air Sport Coupe. Owner: Dan Mamsen. Left: The 1966 Oldsmobile Cutlass Holiday. Owner: Carol Urban. Below: 1969 Dodge Coronet R/T.

Here's a car that teaches a valuable lesson: don't forget lesser versions of a prime collectible. In the case of mid- to late-1950s Buicks, collector interest has usually centered on the Century models, which combined the smaller Buick body with the more powerful engines from the bigger Super and Roadmaster series. This has left the less expensive Special offerings largely ignored, even though they have exactly the same desirable qualities except for maximum rated horsepower and therefore performance.

But there is a happy bonus: the Specials sell for much less than equivalent Centurys on today's market, and this makes them worthy collectibles for those on a more restricted budget.

Price has not been a big worry for Tom Lorek of Elmhurst, Illinois, who

has invested some $7500-$8000 to make this '56 Special Riviera hardtop coupe a three-time winner in class at national Buick club meets. Though some 114,000 of this one model were built, Tom says finding parts is more difficult and costly for all

junior Buicks, perhaps because more of them have been wrecked over the years than the senior cars. Two of his main problems were the specific rear bumper for the car's dual exhausts and the matching door panels for its fairly rare Custom Deluxe

3156

upholstery option. The car also carries optional "Sonomatic" radio, electric clock, and full wheel covers, for which Tom paid $90 but has been offered $250. Finished in authentic Tahiti Coral and Dover White two-tone paint, the car now shows 75,000 total miles.

No, it's not for sale. The last offer Tom had for it—and refused—was a cool $9000.

Automobile Nameplates:
A Fascinating Collectible

by Karl S. Zahm

Few of us have enough funds, space or even the inclination to amass a large number of collectible automobiles. But it's the rare enthusiast indeed who does not possess some type of collectible automobile memorabilia. Radiator badges or nameplates are just one facet of this fascinating segment of the old-car hobby.

Emblems come in different forms. The first such insignia were maker's plates crafted of brass or steel and attached to the wood sides of early cars. These gave the manufacturer's name, serial number and patent information. Ornate, signature-like script began to be seen around 1905, and radiator grilles were the natural backdrops for these stampings. The largest of these was found on the 1906 Autocar, a nameplate measuring nearly two feet across. By 1910, script began to give way to enamels.

Enamels—or, more correctly, cloisonnés—form the bulk of all automotive emblems in the prewar era. These are often highly detailed, beautifully crafted, and usually multi-colored works of almost jewel-like quality. Expensive to manufacture and rarely used today, the cloisonné badge made its most recent production appearance on the special Collector Edition version of the 1982 Chevrolet Corvette.

In simple terms, a cloisonné emblem is a thin, pre-shaped copper alloy plate that is stamped in a large die press to create designs with raised cloisons or dams. Molten glass of the desired color is used to fill the spaces between the partitions. After being allowed to cool, the surface is ground smooth, polished and plated. Until the 1950s, when plastics took over, most emblems were made by this process, either by the D. L. Auld Company or the Gustav Fox Company,

both of which specialized in this type of work. Other, lesser-known suppliers were Ford Metal Specialties, Ross-Adseal and Bastian Brothers.

Some automakers, such as Stanley or Davis, used a part-enamel emblem on which only the car name was done as a cloisonné. Others, such as Cleveland and Roamer, opted for a simple all-metal nameplate. Two- and even three-piece nameplates have also been used occasionally, and could be found at times on such makes as Cadillac, Diana and Packard. Revised car designs, sometimes introduced in mid-year, often dictated a revised emblem. Thus, it is not uncommon to find two or more distinctly different radiator emblems in a given model year on what was essentially the same car.

The most logical spot for an automaker's emblem in the Twenties and Thirties was the upper portion of the radiator shell, but some companies preferred other locations. Beginning in 1932, for example, Pierce-Arrow's crest was found on the crankhole cover. Graham and Willys-Knight both mounted theirs on the headlight tie-bar for a brief period, while the 1933 Hudson had its emblem combined with the hood mascot. Some makers, such as Buick and Nash, felt compelled to place slightly smaller versions of their radiator emblems both on the steering wheel hub and above the taillight, a practice that would become near universal in the postwar era.

Many "assembled" cars of the early Twenties were so alike in performance and styling that it was mainly the design of their nameplates that set them apart. Had the manufacturers spent as much effort perfecting their products as they did creating eye-catching emblems, some may well have survived far longer. The nearly

1

2

3

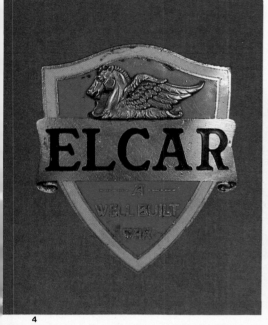

4

8

5

6

7

9

1—**Columbia Six (1919):** Aside from pioneering the cooling system thermostat, this $995 car was quite ordinary. Its best year was 1923 when 6000 cars were built, but the firm ceased operations the next year.

2—**LaFayette (1922):** This independent producer of V-8 luxury cars was founded in Mars Hills, Indiana, in 1920. Two years later it was acquired by Nash Motors and production was transferred to Milwaukee. The marque disappeared after 1924, only to be revived 10 years later as Nash's companion make. This emblem is highly regarded for its cameo-style simplicity.

3—**Crawford (1920):** One of the least remembered names in industry annals, the Crawford was built from 1902 through 1924. Typical production averaged but 25 units annually. 4—**Elcar (1926):** The successor to the earlier Pratt, this make reached its peak in 1919 when some 3500 cars were sold. The insignia is notable for its use of the winged Pegasus from Greek mythology, as well as the prideful slogan. 5—**Duesenberg (1929):** This marque's winged-eagle insignia remains among the most recognizable and revered automotive symbols to this day. Although Duesenberg Motor Car Company was founded in 1920, its most memorable models—the J and supercharged SJ—didn't appear until 1929. But they were too costly for the Depression, and the firm closed its doors in 1937. 6—**Leach (1921):** Doomed to extinction because of its staggering $5500 price, the Leach was one of the few cars made in California, hence that state's traditional big bear symbol in the badge. Operations closed after three years and 150 units. 7—**Owen-Magnetic (1919):** This striking nameplate adorned the sharply vee'd radiator of this luxury car featuring the unusual Entz-built magnetic transmission and a 500-cid six. The O-M vanished in 1922 after only three years. 8—**Playboy (1948):** Fred Astaire may have inspired the badge on this three-passenger convertible, priced at $985 and notable for its retractable metal top. As one of the earliest postwar compacts, however, the Playboy failed to find a market, and only about 100 were completed from 1946 through 1951. 9—**Crow-Elkhart (1919):** A distinctive heart-shaped badge marked these cars from Elkhart, Indiana. They were rather dull machines, though, and the marque vanished after 1924.

10

11

12

forgotten 1916 Moline Dreadnought is a case in point. Although an unimaginative little car, its nameplate was stunning. It was a relatively large piece dominated by a golden battleship at the top; the car's name is shown below, almost as an afterthought. Perhaps the top honors for nameplate artistry should go to the Wills Sainte Claire, one of the more advanced but short-lived cars of the 1920s. No name appears on the insignia, only a lone Canadian goose flying high above a still blue lake bordered by the tops of stately pine trees seen in silhouette.

Every conceivable crown, crest, banner and heraldic figure it seems has been pressed into service over the years to lend a royal imprimatur to all sorts of cars. Lions, pelicans, horses, dragons and other animals have also graced many a nameplate, and one memorable emblem used by Velie even sported a cow's head. Eagles, and their stylized wings in particular, were very popular subjects and remain so today. Reo, Stutz, LaSalle and Playboy are just a few of the many marques that have worn some form of a wing in their nameplates.

Advertising slogans—sometimes amusing, sometimes serious—have also been frequently incorporated in emblems. Making certain all knew it, Kissell stated somewhat obviously that its product was "Every Inch a Car", while the makers of the King billed theirs as "The Car of No Regrets." "The Little Aristocrat" identified the Empire, the Anderson was "A Little Higher In Price, But Made In Dixie" and the badge on the Elcar

proclaimed it "The Well-Built Car".

Extraordinary cars have sometimes sported rather ordinary emblems. For example, the 1929 version of the Duesenberg, America's king of the classics, had only a small, non-enamel badge on the peak of its radiator shell. The very expensive Crane-Simplex of a decade earlier carried only a severely plain brass triangle with embossed lettering. Conversely, some pretty dull machines have worn some of the most interesting and appealing nameplate designs, as the accompanying photos so graphically illustrate.

Considering that there have been over 2000 different makes of automobiles over the past 90 years, the collector who wants to have one nameplate for each make and model would find the total easily exceeding 70,000. Because achieving this goal is next to impossible, most collectors tend to specialize. Some prefer script or maker's plates, others opt for those from commercial vehicles or foreign makes only, and still others are addicted to a specific marque or particular groups of cars like the U.S. muscle machines of the '60s. A few hobbyists, including this author, are content with a single example for each marque. The majority of collectors concentrate on domestic cars and, because of their beauty, tend to favor enamels over other varieties.

The serious collector dates each piece in his collection and usually records the model or series on which it was used. Naturally, the only sure way to authenticate such information is by referring to literature of the period. This includes catalogs, brochures,

and photos issued by the manufacturers as well as trade journals, ads, and other "independent" sources.

Reproduction emblems and nameplates are readily available for some makes and models and, in most cases, are superior in quality to the originals. Restorers tend to prefer them, as they are cheaper, easier to obtain, and look new. Further, it's difficult to tell most copies from the real thing without close inspection using a magnifying glass. An original piece often carries the maker's name or logo stamped in the reverse of the backing plate. Old solder residue, unusual mountings and SAE threads are also indications of the genuine article. However, few serious nameplate collectors will accept the "repro" no matter how well executed it may be, mainly because the aura of the original can never quite be captured in a replica.

Unhappily, the future of nameplate collecting is limited for those just starting out. Most junkyards have long ago been picked clean—not only of emblems but of mascots, hubcaps, and other items even remotely collectible—and worn-out cars that at one time dotted the landscape have been baled into scrap. Even flea markets are less useful than they used to be, more like used car lots than the tantalizing treasure troves we once knew. However, valuable and desirable emblems are still waiting to be discovered, though they're becoming progressively more difficult to find. If you're patient and have a lot of perserverance, this can be a pleasurable and maybe even profitable adjunct to your enjoyment of old cars.

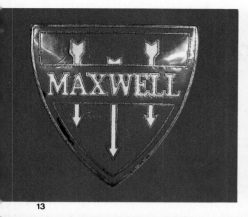

13

17

14

18

20

15

19

21

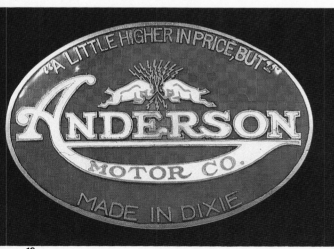

16

10—Kaiser (1948): The buffalo was appropriate for the hard-charging tycoon who founded this new postwar make in 1947. **11—Frazer (1948):** Joseph W. Frazer's family crest appears on this huge badge. The motto *Je Suit Pret* means "I am ready." **12—Nash 8 (1931):** This Art Deco-style badge graced the beautifully styled Twin-Ignition Eights. **13—Maxwell (1923):** This badge appeared in Maxwell's last year as an independent before Walter P. Chrysler's buy-out. **14—Staver (1913):** A former buggy maker built this car in a Chicago suburb from 1907 to 1914. **15—Flanders (1911):** Priced at about $1000, this four-cylinder model carried a very British-looking medallion. **16—Anderson (1921):** Built in Roch Hill, North Carolina in 1916-26, this make enjoyed modest success, but only in its local region. **17—Imperial (1913):** A very regal insignia adorned this car from Jackson, Michigan built in 1907-15. **18—Krit (1911):** Considered by the firm to be the Hopi good luck symbol, the swastika on this badge predates the Nazi era by some 20 years. **19—Stutz (1926):** Formed in 1911, this Indianapolis automaker is best remembered for its romantic Bearcat of the mid-Teens. The make disappeared after 1935. **20—Marathon (1911):** This was another southern make, built in both Jackson and Nashville, Tennessee, in 1908-15. Predictably, the badge employs an Olympic runner. **21—Wills Sainte Claire (1925):** One of the loveliest badges adorned this advanced V-8 car built in Marysville, Michigan.

Attention,
Bargain Hunters...

Friends, are you tired of collector cars only J.R. Ewing could afford? Does the thought of scouring swap meets for off-the-wall parts make you break out in hives? Do you call the weather bureau every time you open that garage door? Are you so bored with your everyday car you find yourself nodding off just backing out of the driveway? If you answered yes to any of these questions, step right this way to the *Collectible Automobile*™ bargain basement, home of the "blue light specials."

What we'll be covering in this column are the irregulars, the factory seconds, the blems of the old-car hobby, the models too numerous to have garnered much, if any, enthusiast interest—the ones that probably never will be high-demand items. We're talking about the unmentioned, the unappreciated, the unexciting: cars like the original Pontiac Grand Am, low-line Corvairs, slant-six Darts, BMW 1600s, and all the rest. Not surprisingly you hardly ever see cars like this written up in hobby publications.

And that's one reason why this obviously classy new magazine has a department called Cheap Wheels. Here's where we try to steer you to

those interesting not-quite-collectibles that make practical alternatives to more modern iron as daily drivers. Compared to the truly rare, high-status collector cars, Cheap Wheels are much less expensive to buy, restore, and maintain; still enjoy wide parts and service availability—and reasonable prices; and are not so precious that you'd worry much about trusting one to heavy traffic or foul weather. In short, these are cars you can really have fun with instead of just preserve. Many have a good reputation for mechanical reliability. Some offer good styling, unusual or desirable features, good gas mileage, even good go in some cases. And, most importantly, Cheap Wheels have the same sort of character that marks the bona fide collectibles, the kind that's seemingly been engineered out of today's cars in this age of electronic gimmickry, computer-aided design, robot welders, and high-tech plastics.

Cheap Wheels fall into two, rather self-evident classes, with some overlap between them. One is what we'll call the "Poor Relations." These are lesser versions of a more sought-after model, sharing the same basic design but fitted with a less powerful engine or less glitzy trim. The 1956 Buick Special Riviera two-door hardtop shown in one of this issue's Photo Features is a splendid example. Not as much horsepower or performance as the traditionally more valued Century, but every bit its equal in virtually every other way. Or, how about an early Mustang with a *six* instead of one of the V-8s collectors prefer? Again, less power, less performance, but in return you get better gas economy, better-balanced handling, easier serviceability, and the very real advantage of being able to run on leaded regular. Sixties' muscle cars are still hot in more ways than one, but how many of them would you really want to drive much on the street? And is there any less tangible appeal in a Plymouth Satellite compared to a GTX or Road Runner, or an Olds Cutlass compared to a 4-4-2?

Low production, good performance, and bargain prices today make the Pontiac Grand Am a good "cheap wheels" choice. Just 8691 of these 1973 four-doors were built.

This is the column for those of you who'd like to drive an interesting older car but don't want to worry about it breaking down or taking a big bite out of your wallet. Cheap Wheels have the same sort of character that marks the bona fide collectibles, but aren't so rare and costly that you'd be afraid to use one as a daily driver. They're also an easy way to get into the hobby.

We could go on for days, but you get the idea: just look around the model line surrounding a really sought-after car. Chances are you'll find a good many siblings with similar entertainment value plus greater practicality for today's driving conditions, all for less dough.

This brings us to the other kind of Cheap Wheels, which we'll call the "Black Sheep." These are cars history doesn't record as being particularly noteworthy when new, so we tend to forget them now. A good many people would undoubtedly say most cars of the '70s qualify here. The '58 Chevrolet Impala used to be thought of this way, though not any more (see "The Forgotten Hot One" feature this issue). Collectors long ago immortalized Studebaker's 1953-54 "Loewy coupes" and their Hawk descendants, but has anybody bothered much with the nicely styled '56 Presidents, for example? And what of the comfortable, roomy, long-wheelbase Lark Cruiser, always overshadowed by its Daytona contemporaries yet ostensibly the top of the passenger-car

line from 1961 right up through Stude's demise in 1966?

There's a whole flock of Black Sheep cars. The smooth 1963-64 Rambler Classic and Ambassador come to mind, especially the limited-edition '64 hardtops. The handsome full-size Ford XLs of 1965-70 have long been neglected in the rush to the "Total Performance" 1963-64 cars, yet some of them are quite rare and the '65s dominated NASCAR. The 1973-75 Pontiac Grand Am wasn't a huge success, partly because of its odd looks, but it was a serious attempt at a European-style high-performance sedan and it delivered the goods. The import ranks are filled with Black Sheep. The first-generation Toyota Celicas and the flawed but eager rotary-engine Mazdas of the same era (especially the Cosmo coupe) are just two of the interesting, yet-to-be-appreciated cars from Japan.

Well, that's the territory. Of course, it's always possible one of our Cheap Wheels may cross over at some point in the future to become a rare and/or sought-after car, appreciating greatly in value as it does. This means you might want to gamble that you can recover some of the money you invest in a model that shows signs of being a "sleeper," especially if you're fond of it to begin with. We're not necessarily going to encourage that because, again, the main purpose of this column is to help you have fun with those older cars that won't cost a bundle to have fun with. By and large, these are not the sort of cars that deserve to be enshrined in museums. A good many lower-eschelon models of the late '60s and early '70s with low- to mid-line engines can be driven and enjoyed today without much regard for sudden attrition that would tend to send their prices skyward. And, of course, supply means nothing without considering demand.

One thing's for sure: we intend to challenge your thinking and get you talking with this column, which we hope will be just as much fun as the cars themselves. In the months to come you'll find something in this space for every taste, every pocketbook. And if you're the type who says "I wouldn't be caught *dead* in one of those," just remember even Elizabeth Taylor shops the sales. *Chris Poole*

Cutting This Issue Down To Size

Highlighting collectible kits
and promotional models of
our featured full-size cars

You'd love to have that '58 Impala you spotted recently, but your wife has already decreed that two unfinished restoration projects are enough, especially since they're occupying all your garage space. Or, you're dying to buy your first collectible car, but a personal cash-flow crisis has forced you into a temporary austerity program. Problems such as these are quite common, though they don't mean you can't have the car of your dreams as long as you're willing to start out on a much smaller scale, like 1/25.

We're talking about scale-model cars here. They cost a lot less money than the real thing and you'll never have to spend an evening wrestling with one while lying on a cold concrete floor in an unheated garage, trying to free stubborn bolts from a rusted exhaust system.

Just as the '58 Impala is valued by the automobile collector, the scale model of that same car is valued by

Opposite page: This 1/32nd '56 Mercury Montclair was the only joint AMT-Revell effort. This page, below: a very rare die-cast '39 Mercury coin bank. Center: 1/25th-scale '62 Dodge Polara 500, modified from Jo-Han's Dodge 440 kit. Bottom: Original AMT 1/25th '64 Pontiac Grand Prix kit.

the model-car enthusiast. In kit form, the closer it is to "original condition," the higher its value. Original condition here means still in the box. An unbuilt kit that sold for a couple of dollars in 1958 is probably worth more than $100 and is rarely seen on sale lists. An unpainted kit that has been assembled in stock form will probably be in the $50 range.

Also valued by collectors are promotional models that were authorized by the car manufacturers. These already-built models were sold or distributed through car dealers and many of them ended up in the hands of children as toys. As happens with most toys, they eventually were damaged or destroyed, so mint condition "promos" are often hard to find. The bodies also are prone to warping, which lowers their value. However, a 1958 Impala hardtop promo in excellent condition probably is worth

$75-90 today. AMT issued the official 1958 Chevrolet promotional models in 1/25 scale with friction-type motors. The models were the Impala hardtop (No. 99C), the convertible (No. 777), and the Nomad station wagon (No. 33S).

The year 1958 is an important one for the model car enthusiast because it is the year AMT started its popular line of 1/25 scale kits. Their one-piece bodies were new at that time and were an immediate hit. While they're quite crude compared with today's kits, they were state-of-the-art then. They had no engines, a flat chassis with molded-in detail, and a very basic interior of about three pieces. Extra parts and decals supplied with the kits let the builder choose from three formats: stock, custom, or racing. These kits were really little more than promotional models molded in styrene instead of acetate.

AMT kits of the 1958 Chevy are hard to find, but the ones to look for are No. 7CK (convertible) and No. 7CKHT (hardtop). AMT released another version of the '58 Impala in 1964 in its Trophy Series (No. 2758) that was molded in blue plastic, and came with doors that opened, a well-detailed engine, full and separate chassis, and a number of custom parts designed by George Barris. Besides the stock engine, a tri-carb 409 was provided with the kit. This kit was offered by AMT until 1967, when the number was changed to 2358 and the box art was redone. The model number was changed again in 1968 to T273 and it remained in the line until 1978.

AMT kit enthusiasts have a choice of models in different sizes. MPC produced a 1/20 scale model of the 1968 AMX (No. 2001) that was available through American Motors dealers and sold for only $1.75. It was well

detailed and molded in red plastic, but it had parts only for a stock version. MPC issued 1969 and 1970 AMX kits that contained extra custom and drag racing parts. Decals with the 1969 kit (No. 2002) duplicated the exterior markings of Craig Breedlove's racing AMX that set more than 100 speed records. The 1970 kit (No. 3170) was reissued in near stock form in 1982 (No. 1-3753), but was offered for only a few months and without the stock wheels of the original version. MPC Kits now sell in the $20-30 range generally, with '68 models the most desirable.

AMT sold 1/25 scale models of the AMX that were actually manufactured by Jo-Han. AMT released annual models for 1969 and 1970 (but not for 1968) and models for all three years in its Trophy Series (all Trophy Series kits were numbered T294). While the model number is the same, the box art is different each year. All years came with stock, custom, and funny car equipment.

Jo-Han's records indicate that no true promos were made of the AMX for 1968, though friction models were available in both 1969 and 1970, and they are seldom seen on sale lists.

Jo-Han is expected to reissue in the near future a kit of Shirley Shahan's '69 AMX Super Stock dragster that the company first released in 1971. Jo-Han also reissued a stock version of the '69 under its U.S.A. Oldies Series (No. C-4369) that is still available at hobby shops and from mail order model car dealers. The kit is quite simple, has excellent details and should be a good choice for the novice model car builder. Because kits are still available, original versions aren't that valuable, usually commanding $15-20.

The timeless design of the 1963 Studebaker Avanti was produced in 1/25 scale by AMT In 1965 (No. 2064 in the Trophy Series) as a well-detailed model with doors that opened and

A collection of collectible 1/25th-scale 1958 Impalas. Left: A Sport Coupe built from AMT's reissued kit. Right: A quartet of promos. The silver boot and dash on the convertibles were found only on the dealer-issued promos, not the store versions. Salmon color (top) is authentic and was new to Chevy's chip chart for '58.

Left, from top: Monogram's ¼th '53 Chevy Bel Air kit. AMT's '53 Stude Starliner, a ⅕th kit. AMC dealers sold MPC's ¹/₂₀th '68 AMX kit. Opposite page, top: Still available, AMT's ¹/₁₆th '55 Chevy Bel Air kit. Center: Two rare '56 Buick promos. Bottom: ¹/₂₅th '56 Cadillac Coupe de Ville and dealer '65 Rambler American promos.

custom and racing parts. However, the kit was quite difficult to build and parts didn't fit as well as modelers had come to expect of AMT, so it never became a best seller. The kit was re-issued several times under different numbers but with minimal changes, so even the originals aren't that highly valued. AMT last issued the Avanti under its Reggie Jackson Collectors Series (No. 4181), and some of those may still be on store shelves.

Hardtops were popular with the car-buying public long before they were built as promotional models for the car companies. It wasn't until about 1955 that many promos were built as hardtops, and then it quickly became the preferred body choice among modelers. Perhaps the most interesting model of this type was the 1959 Ford Skyliner by Revell with a working retractable hardtop, the same as the famous car. The Revell kit was 1/25 scale and was one of the last with multi-piece body construction, though it was not that difficult to build. The original kit (No. H-1227) was available into the early Sixties and was quite advanced for its time, and is not out of date today. In addition to the working hardtop, it included driver and passenger figures, well-detailed engine, and multi-piece detailed chassis.

Revell reissued the Skyliner kit in 1975 (No. H-1333), adding "glass" molded to shape as a new feature that wasn't offered with the original. In 1979, this kit was released again under the Advent banner (No. 3112), a budget series that sold very well in the limited number of stores that stocked them. One of the cost-cutting features of the Advent kits was that some came without plated parts. Because the re-issues are quite common, their value seldom is above $10, less without plated parts. An original Skyliner kit also is not as valuable as it should be because of the reissues, and $25 is generally top dollar.   *Dennis Doty*

1984 Pontiac Fiero:
The Modern Milestone

It's cute, it's capable, and it's a sure-fire "keeper" for the year 2000.

Is there any old-car hobbyist alive who hasn't said at least once, "why did I get rid of that?" If you haven't, you probably will. Regrets, missed opportunities, and forlorn hindsight ("if I only knew then what I know now") are as much a part of this game as dirty hands and swap meets.

We got to thinking about this when planning *Collectible Automobile*,™ especially now that Detroit is again turning out some really interesting cars, cars that one day might be as precious and nostalgic as all those '58 Impalas

we threw away. Now it so happens we spend part of our time driving all sorts of new models and reporting on them for other publications of our parent company. And, we thought, why not take advantage of the opportunity to interpret this experience from the collector's point of view?

So, with all due modesty we present—ta da!—Future Collectibles. We expect to generate more than a little controversy here and, in the process, have some fun and (we hope) get all of you really involved with this new magazine. In this department we'll go out on some very long limbs to predict which cars of the present and recent past (within five to seven years) are most likely to be sought-after and preserved in five, 10, 15 years from now. Audacious? You bet. Speculative? Of course. Imprecise? Not exactly. Dull? Never.

The honor of being our literal first choice goes to Pontiac's 1984 Fiero 2M4. (We know, we know, but you Chrysler, Ford, and Corvette fans will just have to wait.) Much has already been written about this exciting two-seater, so we won't rehash its design points here. Suffice it to say that, as a collector car for the year 2000, the Fiero has an impressive list of credentials that make it a sure-fire "keeper," itself a strong argument for buying one. And really, how could it miss? This is not only America's first mid-engine production car but also our first serious attempt at a sports car in the European idiom since the original Corvette appeared over a generation ago.

Some years back, the prestigious Milestone Car Society set down five criteria for awarding Milestone status to various postwar automobiles. The "SEPIC" quintet—Styling, Engineering, Performance, Innovation, and Craftsmanship—is also, we think, a convenient and logical framework for judging collectibility (indeed, all the certified Milestones are generally accepted collectible automobiles). Now, while MCS requires excellence in at least two of the categories, the Fiero arguably qualifies as a Milestone in four, one of the few new U.S. cars in recent memory we can say that about. And it will be five come 1985, when Pontiac will—as everyone knows—boost the Fiero's performance by offering an optional 2.8-liter V-6.

Let's run through the list. With regard to Styling, the Fiero is most often termed "cute," at least by the people we've talked to. We prefer to think of this design as neat and clean, appropriate for the mechanical layout, balanced and purposeful. The mid-engine configuration touches on Innovation. There's also high originality in the "driveable" space-frame, clad with plastic panels that lend themselves easily to future design changes, not to mention being easy

Production Fieros through the end of calendar 1983 were available only in red or white so Pontiac could concentrate on paint quality. These cars seem likely to become the most coveted of the 1984 models. Handsome wheels are standard on the top-line SE.

and cheap to repair. Engineering? Okay, Pontiac did some heavy borrowing from the GM parts bins—*too* heavy say the purists—but where else can you get all-independent suspension and four-wheel disc brakes for less than half the price of an '84 'Vette? Besides, a great many sports cars over the years have shared components with higher-volume family models and it's just as defensible here, especially since Pontiac was concerned not only with keeping prices reasonable but also with reliability in a mechanical layout new for a Detroit producer.

As for Craftsmanship, the cars speak for themselves. Paint finish is quite good, partly due to Pontiac's go-slow production start-up and partly due to the special "in place" painting procedure devised especially for the Fiero's plastic panels. This quality consciousness explains why initial color choices were limited to just red and white which, years from now, will be a sure sign of the earliest production—and thus most desirable—'84 Fieros. Body panel fit is pleasing and true thanks to Pontiac's newly developed "mill and drill" process. And, the much closer cooperation between management and union at the Pontiac home plant, the only facility building the Fiero, really shows in the tight, rattle-free assembly we've seen even on the early production examples.

Performance, as we've implied,

isn't a Fiero forte right now, at least not in a straight line. Even so, the car is smooth, refined, and adequately quick. It's also amazingly quiet for a midships car, a tribute to its body and sound engineering. And handling and roadholding are as terrific as you'd expect from this layout. As for ride comfort, the Fiero is simply a revelation next to the bone-jarring Corvette, civilized and with very little harshness. Who said you can't have good cornering ability *and* a good ride at the same time?

Other drawbacks? We can think of only two. For one, the Fiero will lack exclusivity for a good many years. Pontiac can build up to 100,000 of them annually, and demand is bound to be strong for the first three or four years at least. For another, though they seem destined to become desirable as first of the line, the '84 models will always be denied the aura of high performance that adds so much to a collector car's luster.

Ah, we can hear you skeptics already: "No tradition. No history. Too heavy. Too tame. Hasn't proved itself. It's just a shorty X-car with Chevette steering and not enough trunk space." Maybe. Tell you what: just talk to someone who *used* to own an early Corvette or a two-seat T-Bird. And after they've finished explaining why they were foolish enough to let cars like that slip away, don't be surprised if you're invited for a ride in their new Pontiac Fiero. *Chris Poole*

Book Reviews

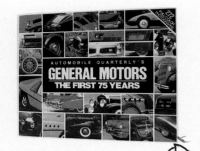

General Motors—The First 75 Years
By The Editors of Automobile Quarterly Magazine
Published by: Crown Publishers, Inc. New York, New York, 224 pages; $24.95

Looking for a car book that's brief on text but big on gorgeous photos? Then take a look at *Automobile Quarterly's* new release, *General Motors—The First 75 Years.*

This slick volume tells GM's history through 385 illustrations, including 272 full-color photographs. The best in automotive masterpieces from General Motors are shown, from its incorporation in 1908 with Buick and Olds up to the 1984 Fiero and Corvette.

Through its pictures, this book dramatically demonstrates the vast diversity in design and engineering that over the decades has made GM the largest auto manufacturer in the world.

We see excellent examples of the pioneering cars of the 1910s, the stately beauty of the elegant '20s and '30s, and the curvaceous bodies of the 1940s and early '50s.

The mid-'50s to 1960s is a wild period, with ever-changing designs in the annual search for the "modern" car with mass market high performance options. The 1970s and part of this decade are also covered, with GM's answers to the new lord of design, energy conservation.

There are glimpses at the bus and truck divisions, nice sections on foreign subsidiaries, and a 74-year production count on all GM marques.

This book obviously was never intended to be the definitive volume on General Motors' long history, but this book provides a fine sense of the impact GM has had on the world of automobiles.

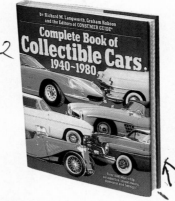

Complete Book of Collectible Cars 1940-1980
By Richard M. Langworth, Graham Robson, and the Editors of CONSUMER GUIDE®
Published by: Publications International, Skokie, Illinois, 384 pages; $14.98

Mild to serious auto hobbyists and investors should take a good gander at *Complete Book of Collectible Cars 1940-1980.*

Here I have found a well conceived and assembled volume that provides the facts needed to make a realistic judgment when considering the purchase of a "special" old car.

Alphabetically arranged are the classic and "coming" American and foreign cars likely to interest American and Canadian collectors. The book is all the more enjoyable because the authors have not only included the well-known and sure-fire collectibles, but are not afraid to leave the beaten path either; the 1961-63 Ford Falcon Futura is included along with the early T-birds.

I liked this book's format, where under the photo of each of the more than 600 cars is listed precise and pertinent information. Helpful facts, such as how many units were produced, engine specs, a brief history, and how much the car is worth today, as well as a five-year projected market value are included.

The clever "For" and "Against" evaluation sections are very useful. Potential buyers should know which models have rust-prone bodies and hard-to-find parts, as well as those vehicles with high appreciation value and timeless designs.

While some auto buffs might feel that the author's findings are a bit subjective, and in the final analysis it will be the public's whim and fancy that make a car valuable, I still recommend this guide as a reference source if you're interested in collecting cars.

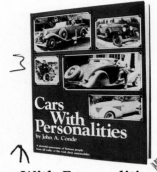

Cars With Personalities
By John A. Conde
Published by: Arnold-Porter, 248 pages; $21.95

Here is a very enjoyable and nostalgic mini history of the automobile, with the famous and near-famous of yore posing with legendary autos in hundreds of contemporary photographs.

John Conde, a top auto historian for over forty years, has assembled a visual collection for the antique auto buff as well as for those intrigued by movie stars, sports heroes, and auto and political greats of the past.

This treasury of snapshots features such characters as W. C. Fields with his 1933 V-12 Lincoln, Babe Ruth standing on the running board of his 1937 Nash Ambassador, and Richard Nixon parading in a 1958 Edsel convertible. The photos are nicely reproduced and under each is included a brief description for every car and celebrity.

Mr. Conde's vast experience and knowledge fills this book with pictorial treats as well as a multitude of trivia. Over 120 different car brands are featured, including Duesenberg, Essex Terraplane, Hupmobile, Shelby Mustangs, etc. Personalities range from Charles Brady King (first automobile driver in Detroit, 1896) to football great O. J. Simpson, with hundreds of others in between.

I recommend *Cars With Personalities* for lighthearted yet informative reading.

Reviewed by Mitch Frumkin

Calendar of Events

Send events to Collectible Automobile,™ 3841 W. Oakton St., Skokie, IL 60076.

April 1, Hillside, IL
Old Town "Escorts" Ltd. Model Car Club Swap Meet. Promotionals, kits, frictions, tin die casts, literature, parts, etc. Holiday Inn, 4400 Frontage Road, Hillside, IL. Adults $2, children under 12 $1. Information: Tom Lima Jr., 1933 North Sedgewick, Chicago, IL 60614; (312) 642-5131 after 6 p.m.

April 5-8, Charlotte, NC
Charlotte '84 Collector Car Flea Market and Car Show. Largest collector car flea market in the southwest. Giant car show Saturday, April 7, hundreds of cars judged in all AACA classes. Free camping. Charlotte Motor Speedway, U.S. Route 29 10 miles north of Charlotte, NC. Information and reservations: Hornets Nest Region, AACA, c/o Mel Carson, 1927 Carmel Ridge Road, Charlotte, NC 28211.

April 6-8, Hershey, PA
Fifth annual Hershey in the Spring Auto Flea Market, Collector Car Mart, Arts & Crafts, and Car Show. Adults $1, children under 12 free. Information and reservations: HITS, PO Box 234, Annville, PA 17003; (717) 867-4810 6-9 pm EST.

April 26-29, Fort Worth, TX
Twelfth annual Pate Museum of Transportation Swap Meet. Third largest swap meet in U.S. Sponsored by South Central Swap Meet Assn., U.S. Route 377, 14 miles south of Fort Worth, TX. Information and reservations: Don Moore, 7751 Cak Vista, Houston, TX 77087.

April 27-29, Rockford, IL
Lewis E. Lazarus' 11th annual April in Rockford. Collector Car Auction, Show, and Swap Meet. Winnebago Exhibition Center, Pecatonica, IL (15 minutes west of Rockford just off U.S. Route 20). Information and reservations: "A in R," Box 368, Forreston, IL 61030; (815) 938-2250/2668 11 to 5 weekdays or 235-9816 after hours.

April 29, South Bend, IN
Twenty-first annual swap meet and antique car show sponsored by Pioneer Auto Assn. Admission $1. 4-H fairgrounds, Jackson Road near Ironwood Road, South Bend. Information: Paul Kohler, 922 E. Jefferson, Mishawaka, IN 46545; (219) 255-5916.

April 29, Greenville, SC
Sixth annual antique and classic auto show and flea market. Sponsored by South Carolina Region AACA and Boy's Home of the South. Admission $2. Roper Mountain (Park) Science Center, Greenville. Information: Dick Keating, PO Box 1043, Easley, SC 29640; (803) 859-8785.

April 29, Jefferson, WI
Seventh annual "Spring Little Carlisle" swap meet and car show. Admission $2. Jefferson Fairgrounds. Information: Madison Classics, 4801 Flint Lane, Madison, WI 53714; (608) 244-8416.

May 13, Glastonbury, CT
Fifteenth annual antique auto show and flea market. Sponsored by Southern New England Region VCCA. Admission $2. Elks Field, Glastonbury. Information: Bob Larson, 570 Deming Road, Berlin, CT 06037; (203) 828-9931.

May 25-27, Atlanta, GA
Atlanta '84 Memorial Weekend Collector Car Flea Market and Car Show, hosted by Atlanta Region AACA and HCCA. Over 1000 outside and 150 inside spaces, low space rental rates. Giant invitational car show Saturday, May 25, with trophies for 40 classes from 1900-1982. North Georgia State Fairgrounds, 2245 Callaway Road, Marietta, GA. Adults $2, children 12 and under free with adult. Information: Harold Turner, 859 Ellis Road, Stone Mountain, GA 30083; (404) 294-7296.

Automobile Puzzle

My uncle Jack has worked for Ace Auto Wreckers for 25 years. Yesterday he drove home in this car. In the last 10 years, he had carefully collected enough parts from hundreds of different makes and models of cars to build the car you see below. It sure looked like a crazy conglomeration, but the thing ran and got great mileage to boot! I enjoyed trying to identify the different cars from which each part had been salvaged. So far, I've come up with 16 different cars. How many can you find? *Answers on page 96*

Value Guide

Year/Make/Model	Restorable	Good	Excellent	5-year Projection	Notes
1970 AMC Rebel Machine	$ 500-1000	$1000-2000	$ 2500-3000	+25%	
1949 Buick Roadmaster Riviera	1000-2000	2500-5000	6500-9000	+75%	
1954-55 Buick Century	750-1250	2500-5000	2500-4250	+25%	
1949 Cadillac Series 62 Coupe de Ville	2000-3000	3500-6000	6000-10,000	+50%	
1950-52 Chevrolet Styleline Deluxe Bel Air	800-1500	1500-2500	3000-5000	+50%	add 10% for 1950 models
1958 Chevrolet Impala Sport Coupe	1000-1800	2000-3500	3500-7500	+25%	
1967-69 Chevrolet Camaro Sport Coupe	400-1000	1500-2500	2400-4500	+50%	add 75% for Z-28, 15% for RS/SS equipment; deduct 25% for sixes
1950 Chrysler Town & Country Newport	3000-4500	4500-9000	10,000-15,000	+75%	
1956 Clipper Custom Constellation	6000-1000	1000-2500	3500-4500	+25%	
1968-71 Continental Mark III	500-1000	1500-3500	400-5000	+25%	
1950 DeSoto Custom Sportsman	500-1000	1500-2500	3000-4500	no change	
1955-56 DeSoto Fireflite Sportsman (2d only)	400-850	1500-3000	3000-4500	+25%	
1950 Dodge Coronet Diplomat	500-1000	1500-2300	3000-4000	+25%	
1968-69 Dodge Dart GTS	500-800	1200-1800	2500-3000	+25%	
1958 Edsel Citation	500-1000	2000-3500	3500-5000	+50%	
1951 Ford Custom Victoria	700-1500	1500-2500	3500-5000	+15%	
1954 Ford Crestline Skyliner	750-1500	2500-3000	4000-5500	+25%	
1955-56 Ford Fairlane	1000-1750	2000-3000	3500-4000	+35%	add 75% for Crown Victoria, 100% for plastic-top C.V.
1957-59 Ford Fairlane 500 Skyliner	1000-2000	3000-4500	5000-7500	+35%	
1965-66 Ford Mustang	500-900	1250-2500	3000-4000	+50%/V-8s +25%/six	add 15% for 271-bhp V-8, 15% for GT package; deduct 15% for six
1951-53 Hudson Hornet Hollywood	600-1800	3000-5000	5000-7500	+50%	add 10% for Twin-H, 50% for 7-X
1955-56 Imperial Newport/ Southampton	600-1350	1750-3000	3000-4000	+35%	
1953-54 Lincoln Capri	500-1250	1250-3500	3500-5000	+25%	
1956-57 Lincoln Premiere	500-1000	1000-2250	3500-5000	+15%	
1954-55 Mercury Sun Valley	1500-2000	3000-5000	6000-9000	+25%	
1957-58 Mercury Turnpike Cruiser	1000-2000	2000-4500	5500-7000	+15%	
1969-70 Mercury Cyclone	750-1500	1500-2250	2250-3000	+25% (+35% Spoiler)	add 15% for CJ, 10% for CT, 35% for Spoiler
1950-52 Nash Rambler Country Country Club	400-800	850-1600	2000-3000	+25%	add 10% for LeMans option; 5% for Custom models
1949 Oldsmobile Futuramic 98 Holiday	1500-2500	2500-3500	3500-5000	+50%	
1955 Oldsmobile Holidays	1000-1500	1500-3000	3000-4500	+15%	
1955-56 Packard Caribbean	1500-2500	3500-6000	6500-10,000	+75%	
1951-52 Plymouth Cranbrook Belvedere	750-1250	1500-2500	3000-4000	no change	
1957-58 Plymouth Fury	1200-1800	2500-3500	3500-5000	+75%	
1964-66 Plymouth Barracuda	350-750	750-1500	2250-3500	+25%	deduct 15% for six
1967 Plymouth Belvedere GTX	800-1300	2000-2700	3000-3700	+25%	
1950 Pontiac Chieftain Catalina	750-1250	2000-3500	3500-5000	+25%	
1962-64 Pontiac Grand Prix	750-1500	2000-3500	3500-5000	+10%	
1957 Rambler Custom Rebel	400-800	1000-2000	2500-3000	+35%	
1952 Studebaker Commander State Starliner	100-1500	2250-3000	3500-4500	+25%	
1953-54 Champion Regal Regal Starliner	600-1500	2000-3000	3000-4500	+75%	
1952-54 Willys Aero-Eagle	500-1000	1000-1750	2500-3000	+25%	

Automobile Puzzle Answers

1. Top—1966 AMC Marlin
2. Windshield—1956 Chrysler
3. Spoiler—1970 Charger Daytona
4. Rear Fender—1955 Chevrolet Bel Air
5. Door—1958 Thunderbird
6. Right Fender—1974 Chevrolet Monte Carlo
7. Hood Scoop—1954 Mercury
8. Hood—1953 Studebaker
9. Left Grille—1954 Studebaker
10. Right Grille—1953 Studebaker
11. Left Fender—1957 Nash
12. Bumper—1968 Corvette
13. Left Lower Grille—1970 Corvette
14. Right Lower Grille—1968 Corvette
15. Front hub cap—1953 Studebaker
16. Rear hub cap—1957 Ford